Hardtack
— *and* —
Haversacks

BY
STEVEN W. SILER
AUTHOR OF THE BEST-SELLING *Signature Tastes* SERIES

A **Tastes in Time**™ SERIES BOOK

To Gina Siler Simpson,

for her most gracious assistance with this book,

but moreso for planting in me a love of the South

and history of the War Between the States.

Copyright ©2014 by Smoke Alarm Media

ALL RIGHTS RESERVED. No part of this book may be reproduced or transmitted in any form by any means, unless you have a note from your mother giving you permission. In lieu of a note, please contact Smoke Alarm Media at 2950 Newmarket Place, Bellingham, WA 98226.

Layout by Steven W. Siler

Photography collected by Rosalie Anne Fradella and team, except where noted. A special thanks to the Library of Congress archives, Wikipedia and National Archives for their photography.

You can find us at www.SmokeAlarmMedia.com

Siler, Steven W.

Hardtack and Haversacks: Recipes and Their Stories of American Civil War

ISBN 978-1503068261

1. Cookery-History-American Civil War

Printed in the United States of America

Everything in the eating line is what we care the most about, so you may send me plenty of butter, some sausage, a piece of ham or chicken, some buckwheat flour, crullers, cake, pepper, saleratus, dried fruit, hard boiled eggs, a loaf of bread, chestnuts and some onions stuck in the corner of the box... I have often heard that hunger was a good cook but I never realized it until I came in the army.

Letter from Union soldier
Alonzo Bryant Searing to his family

The Recipes

A Delicious Sauce...........7	Lemonade...........97
Apple Dumplings...........9	Loaf Cake Without Eggs...........99
Apple Jelly...........11	Lobster Salad...........101
Apple Pie...........13	Macaroni...........103
Bachelor's Loaf...........15	Malina Pie...........105
Beef Kidney Rognon de boeuf suberbe...........17	Maryland Biscuits...........107
Biscuits...........19	Medicines...........109
Black Pudding...........21	Mint Julep...........1i1
Bologna Sausage...........23	Molasses Cookies...........113
Buckwheat Cakes...........25	New Orleans Gumbo...........115
Calf's Feet Fricasseed...........27	New Years Cookies...........117
Calico Dye...........29	Okra Soup...........119
Casserole of Rice...........31	Oysters...........121
Cherry Bread...........33	Peas Pudding...........123
Chicken Fricassee...........35	Pepper Sauce...........125
Chili Pepper Sauce...........39	Pickled Green Tomatoes...........127
Chocolate Cake...........41	Picollilly...........129
Clam Soup...........43	Pigeons in Jelly...........131
Cod...........45	Pillaff...........133
Coffee Syrup...........47	Plain Pound Cake...........135
Cold Slaw...........49	Plum Pudding...........137
Confederate Pudding...........51	Plum Wine...........139
Cottage Cheese...........53	Popovers...........141
Crullers...........55	Porter Beer...........143
Cucumbers...........57	Potato Pudding...........145
Cure for Camp Itch...........59	Pumpkin Pie...........147
Delicious Brown Bread...........61	Rabbit and Oyster Fricasee...........149
Delmonico's Chocolate Pudding...........63	Republican Fruit Cake...........151
Eel Soup...........65	Republican Inaugural Ball...........153
Elder Wine...........67	Rhubarb Jam...........155
Flannel Cake...........69	Rice Cake...........157
Fruitcake...........71	Sally Lunn...........159
Gherkins...........73	Salt Pork...........161
Gingerbread...........75	Sausage...........163
Green Corn Pudding...........77	Southern Rolls...........165
Hair Tonic...........79	Split Pea Soup...........167
Ham & Chicken Pie...........81	Sweet Journey Cake...........169
How to Cook Pig's Head...........83	Sweet Potato Pone...........171
Indian Loaf...........85	Syllabub...........173
Italian Syrup...........87	Tomato Ketchup...........175
Jelly Beans...........89	Turtle...........177
Jubal Early Punch...........91	Vegetable Soup...........179
Kisses...........93	Washington Breakfast Cake...........181
Lady Baltimore Cake...........95	White Puddings...........183

A Delicious Sauce

THE IMPROVED HOUSEWIFE
BY A.L. WEBSTER (1851)

> A Delicious Sauce.
>
> Claret wine, or good Port, one pint; half a pint of walnut pickle; three fresh lemon peels, thinly sliced; peel and slice six eschalots; scrape or grate three large spoonsful of fresh horse-radish, half an ounce of allspice and the same of pepper corns powdered, two Chili peppers chopped and a teaspoonful of celery seed. Put all these into a wide-mouthed bottle, and pour on them a pint of mushroom catsup; shake well and cork tightly. In fourteen days, it is fit for use. This is a delightful and really economical seasoning for broths, stews, and sauces, as a little answers in drawn butter or gravies. No housekeeper should be without it.

The primary ingredient in this delicious sauce is Port Wine. While wonderful to drink and an excellent addition to any meal, it was also used during the Civil War as a medicine to help treat soldiers. As a Union medic reported many years after the war,

"During a campaign our stock of medicines was necessarily limited to standard remedies, among which could be named opium, morphine, Dover's powder, quinine, rhubarb, Rochelle salts, castor oil, sugar of lead, tannin, sulphate of copper, sulphate of zinc, camphor, tincture of opium, tincture of iron, tincture opii, camphorate, syrup of squills, simple syrup, alcohol, whiskey, brandy, port wine, sherry wine, etc." In fact, alcoholic beverages were seen like a tonic for those who may be in shock, wounded or recovering from surgery. Even the healthy soldiers were given the occasional ration of whiskey to give them good health during the long hauls.

Amish cart shop, Pennsylvania

Apple Dumplings

MRS HALE'S NEW COOK BOOK
SARAH JOSEPHA HALE (1857)

BAKED APPLE DUMPLINGS.

Prepare a paste as for boiled dumplings; only instead of one large one, make several small ones; avoid lapping the paste, as much as possible, after the fruit is introduced; butter the pan in which they are baked, to prevent their sticking; lay the folded side down; bake three-quarters of an hour; serve hot; eaten with cream.

Most cultures, including Scandinavian, Italian, British & Japanese heritages all have a version of a sweet fruit dumpling they use as desserts. While some dumpling wraps may be thick and a major part of the dish, still others may only be a thin covering where the inside is the treat to be anticipated. Various countries prepare their dumplings in different manners, with some frying their dumplings while others steam, simmer or bake them. In America, German immigrants, most notably the Amish, were know for their apple streudels and dumplings. Settling in Pennsylvania and Ohio River Valley, the Amish did not take an active combatant's role in the conflict but did offer food and shelter to both armies, most notably in the Gettysburg campaign. Because of the indepedent lifestyle means of their culture, many Amish communities did not suffer the food shortages that would affect other parts of the nation.

Max Lieberman, *Canning Factory*

Apple Jelly

HANDWRITTEN FAMILY RECIPE
CIVIL WAR ERA

Happy was the solider that had a sweetheart, wife or mother at home to send him goodies to make the bland, monotonous daily meals a bit sweeter. One such treasure was indeed apple jelly or truly any jelly for that matter. While most good southern cooks made their own homemade jellies to send their soldiers, a part of northern Vermont was home to the commercial apple-growing region and saw the start up of a jelly factory in Marshfield, VT by two industrious employees with a $1,000 investment. The apple of choice was the McIntosh apple. James Hunter, a solider in the 2nd Colorado Infantry went home from the war to start a manufacturing plant in Vermont that ended up a successful business by producing eight to ten tons of jelly every season.

11

Civil War Post Office

Apple Pie

*DIRECTIONS FOR COOKING BY THE TROOPS
BY FLORENCE NIGHTINGALE (1861)*

Apple Pie.

Fill a pudding dish with pared and cored apples—the tart baking apple; fill each hole of the apple with good brown sugar; cut very thinly the oily part of the rind of two lemons; then cut it into narrow strips, and lay on the top of the apples; squeeze the juice of the lemons into a cup and add a little cold water; pour this over the apples, and sprinkle over more sugar, quite thickly; then cover the whole with a nice puff paste, and bake it rather slowly one hour; serve hot. Peaches are very nice done in the same way, with the stones left in and only pared, but no lemon, and very little water as they make their own juice.

While it's certain that any solider would have preferred the real thing, mock apple pies were common treats made by soldiers during the Civil War. Due to the blockade and lack of good fruits to many of the men, a recipe developed that used their rations to duplicate a homemade favorite. It actually had no apples in the recipe at all but hard tack was substituted along with sugar syrup for sweetness. The end product comes remarkably close to the original, although it's a bit saltier than one might be used to. When served with ice cream, it's hardly distinguishable from the original. This recipe re-surfaced again in the 20th century as Ritz Crackers published a recipe on their boxes for American's to try. So maybe the saying should be, 'As American as Cracker Pie."

Tyler Huffman, like many veterans, had to wait until after the war to marry.

Bachelors Loaf

MRS HALE'S NEW COOK BOOK
SARAH JOSEPHA HALE (1857)

> **BACHELOR'S LOAF.**
>
> Pour on three-fourths of a pound of sifted corn-meal one pint of boiling hot new milk; stir well together; then beat the white and yolk of three eggs separately, reserving the white for the last ingredient added; add a little salt, and a spoonful of lard; the whole to be beaten quite light. Grease the pans, pour in the above, and bake one hour.

The average solider was indeed a bachelor during the Civil War. Of the 2.75 million soldiers who fought, 2 million Yankees and 750,000 Rebs, their statistics were remarkably similar. According to historian Bell I. Wiley, the solider on both sides had several things in common. They were white, born in America, a farmer, protestant and single. On the whole, the majority served in the infantry, were between the ages of 18 and 29, stood on average 5'8" tall and weighed about 143 lbs. You can bet they were a might site slimmer when they came walking home from the war. The Bachelor's loaf is so named because of its smaller size that eliminated waste and can even be bought in stores today if you're so inclined. It tastes fantastic with a little bit of that apple jelly spread on top.

A Bachelor's cupboard

Cattle running amuck while being driven north.

Beef Kidney Rognon de Boeuf Suberbe

THE IMPROVED HOUSEWIFE
BY A.L. WEBSTER (1851)

> BEEF KIDNEY, ROGNON DE BŒUF SUPERBE.—FRIED.
>
> Remove all the fat and the skin from the kidney, and cut it in slices moderately thin. Mix with a teaspoonful of salt, grated nutmeg and cayenne pepper. Sprinkle over them this seasoning, and also parsley and eschalot, chopped very fine. Fry them over a quick fire until brown on both sides, pour into a cup of good gravy a glass of Madeira, and when the slices of the kidney are browned, pour it into the pan gradually; just as it boils throw in a spoonful of lemon juice, with a piece of butter the size of a nut. Have ready a dish, garnished with fried bread cut in dice; pour the whole into it.

As time passed the essentially pastoral character of Southern agriculture became more heavily a plow and commercial system. The plantation system, small family farming, and the range cattle industry expanded rapidly between 1836 and the Civil War. Annual cattle drives were being made from points in south central Texas south and east along the Opelousas Trail to New Orleans, and on the Old Government Road to Little Rock and Fort Smith, Arkansas; and on other trails or extensions to Alexandria and Shreveport, Louisiana, or Natchez and Vicksburg, Mississippi. In 1846 Edward Piper drove a herd of Texas cattle to Ohio. In the 1850s Texas herds were being driven to Chicago and Illinois markets, to California, and to railheads in Iowa. The value of livestock on Texas farms rose from about $10.5 million to $43 million between 1850 and 1860.

Keebler Baking, the same company as present day, baked biscuits for the Union.

BISCUITS

*CONFEDERATE RECEIPT BOOK
BY WEST AND JOHNSTON, RICHMOND (1863)*

> BISCUIT.—Take one quart of flour, three teaspoonfuls of cream of tartar, mixed well through the flour, two tablespoonfuls of shortening, one teaspoonful of soda, dissolved in warm water, of a sufficient quantity to mould the quart of flour. For large families the amount can be doubled.

This delicious recipe is nothing like the biscuits the soldiers received in their rations during the Civil War. While some called them biscuits, the majority of the men called them hardtack. Hardtack is more similar to a cracker and it was inexpensive and lasted a long time in storage, making it especially popular to the military. Some of the 3x3" crackers that the boys in blue and gray received had been in storage since the mid 1840s and the days of the Mexican-American war. Because of the insect infestation, many soldiers would crumble the biscuit into their coffee so that the bugs could be skimmed off the top. Still others would simply eat their rations in the dark under the old adage that "what you can't see won't hurt you."

FRYING HARDTACK.

Sausage packing plant for Philip Armour.

Black Pudding

MRS HALE'S NEW COOK BOOK
SARAH JOSEPHA HALE (1857)

Black Puddings.

Stir three quarts of sheep's blood with one spoonful of salt till cold, boil a quart of very fine homony in sufficient water to swell them until cooked, drain, and add them to the blood with a pound of suet, a little pounded nutmeg, some mace, cloves, and allspice, a pound of the hog's fat cut small, some parsley finely minced, sage, sweet herbs, a pint of bread crumbs, salt, and pepper; mix these ingredients well together, put them into well cleaned skins, tie them in links, and prick the skins, that while boiling they may not burst. Let them boil twenty minutes, and cover them with clean straw until they are cold.

"Revenge is Black Pudding."
— All Quiet on the Western Front

Whether you call it black pudding, blood pudding or blood sausage, it's a sure bet that this dish is no pudding or dessert at all. In actuality, it's a sausage that is made by combining the blood of an animal, in this case, a sheep, with a filler ingredient like hominy, as used in this recipe. Other filler ingredients a cook might bring to the pot include oatmeal, barley, chestnuts, onions, or sweet potatoes. Because meat was hard to come by in the Civil War days, the vegetable fillers were used instead. Most likely, this recipe came over with the huge German contingent of immigrants who introduced the Americas to Blutwurst or blood sausage, although, there are English, Irish and Australian recipes for a similar dish.

Lincoln reviewing the 34th New York, the famous "Garibaldi Guard" of Italian Americans.

Bologna Sausage

MRS HALE'S NEW COOK BOOK
SARAH JOSEPHA HALE (1857)

Bologna Sausages.

Chop very finely ten pounds of lean, juicy beef, two pounds and a half of fat fresh pork cut into very small pieces with a knife—not chopped—a quarter of an ounce of pounded mace, the same of pounded cloves, and two ounces of ground black pepper; mix these well, stuff this mixture lightly into the straight gut of the beef; make each one about twelve inches in length and tie both ends closely. Put them into a ham brine for four or five days, and then press it for a day or two to make it firm, and smoke for a week. They must be kept in a dry place, and improve by age, and when a year old they are excellent.

"A manufacture of bologna sausage accused a man whom he had discharged of spreading a report that the manufacturer's sausage was made of dog meat. The accused man protested: I never said any such thing, but I will tell you what I did say. I said that where bologna sausages are plentiful, dogs are scarce."

—Sam Houston

No, they weren't made of dog meat as the Texas' most famous citizen suggested in his humorous quip, but the were definitely plentiful after the Civil War brought together soldiers of varying ethnicities. Italian by heritage, these sausages would never have made it into an early 1800s American cookbook. But with the sharing of foods with soldiers from all walks of life and backgrounds over a campfire, ethnic foods that American gentlemen might never have discovered were instead shared and enjoyed together.

David Benedict, Canadian Abenaki Indian who raised buckwheat to be sold to the Union

Buckwheat Cakes

MRS HALE'S NEW COOK BOOK
SARAH JOSEPHA HALE (1857)

Buckwheat Cakes.

Take as much warm water as you will require for the size of the family, thicken this with good buckwheat to a fritter batter, add a teaspoonful of salt if two quarts is made, two handsful of corn meal, and one wine glass of good yeast; it is much better made with boiled milk; but be careful to let the milk be only warm, not to scald the yeast, or they will be heavy.

"I had a dream de odder night
When ebery ting was still;
I thought I saw Susanna,
A coming down de hill.
De buckwheat cake war in her mouth,
The tear was in her eye,
Says I'm coming from de South,
Susanna, don't you cry."
—Stephen Foster

A native of China, the buckwheat pancake traveled a long way to become a staple of both sides of the United States. Griddle cakes made from the buckwheat flour are brown, tasty and nutritious. As a breakfast food, they helped the farmer or soldier begin his day with a large and filling meal. Different regions called them by various names, with the south laying claim to buckwheat cakes and the north referring to them as griddle cakes.

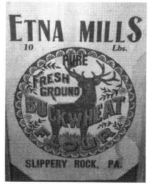

TINSHOP CREW
Winslow's Cannery Portland, M

Calfs Feet Fricasseed

THE IMPROVED HOUSEWIFE
BY A.L. WEBSTER (1851)

> **Calves' Feet Fricasseed (Pieds de veau en Fricassee.)**
>
> Soak them three hours, simmer them in equal proportions of milk and water, until they are sufficiently tender to remove the meat from the bones, in good sized pieces. Dip them in yolk of egg, cover with fine bread crumbs; pepper and salt them, fry a beautiful brown, and serve in white sauce.

If one thing can be said about our forefathers and mothers it's that they were most definitely resourceful. Certainly, they left little to waste. So was the case with the cow and the abundance of recipes available for calves' feet. There are recipes from the era that stew, bake, and boil the feet with varying accompanying ingredients. Additional recipes show the intrepid cook how to make the much needed calf's feet broth as well as calf's foot jelly, a dessert delicacy of the time. The purpose of the calves' feet was not to send a meaty taste to the dessert, but to act as a gelatin to set the jelly. The calves' feet could also be used in a delicious soup to warm up a cold day, something the traveling solider would definitely appreciate.

Sewing school, Columbus, Ohio 1861

Calico Dye

HANDWRITTEN FAMILY RECIPE
CIVIL WAR ERA

This is a rather unique recipe from George Haworth recipe book, a printer's book for fabric colors! The recipes are accompanied by a fabric sample, pasted onto the page. The colors and patterns shown vary greatly but the process is often very similar, many times referring the reader back to a previous color for instruction. They have names such as "olive for block," "steam purple," and "wash of pinks for blacks." Ingredients used include bark, berry liquids, pot ash, vinegar, water, nitrate of copper, and flour. Different colors required different boiling times, resting times, and finishing methods. Varying chemical reactions would yield different shades of the same color. The instructions also detail which recipes to follow to achieve the red and gold shades. This particular cloth was prepared for steam work.

Slave with rice basket and fruit.
Charleston, SC

Casserole of Rice

MRS HALE'S NEW COOK BOOK
SARAH JOSEPHA HALE (1857)

Casserole of Rice.

Use what is called a "well mould," either of tin or earthen ware; cook with care as directed for Croquettes, a quarter of a pound rice, and instead of frying press the rice when cooked into the mould; have the centre free, and into that put some nicely stewed tart apples, then on the top again put some of the prepared rice; this must be done while it is warm, and have the mould quite full; it must have been wet with milk to prevent the rice from sticking; keep this hot until wanted for table, then turn it out on the dish. Serve hot.

Make no mistake, this recipe is a different dish all together from any rice casserole you may have had in the past. Instead of being a large mixture of rice and other vegetables, here you have a pretty dessert confection that is rice surrounding stewed apples. By using plenty of milk in the recipe, the rice can conform to the shape of the mould, but still come loose intact and in the design of the mould. Granny Smith apples are the apple of choice for many when making this unusual, by today's standards, dessert. This is considered a warm and delicious dessert for a cold winter's night and was very popular on Christmas menus of the day. Rice coquettes are another similar recipe popular during the holidays, wedding dinners and other fine dining experiences.

A fruit canning factory of the time.

Cherry Bread

*HANDWRITTEN FAMILY RECIPE
CIVIL WAR ERA*

> Cherry bread.
> Pick the stalks from 2 lbs. of cherries, put them in a preserving pan with about a pint of claret or port wine & 3/4 lb. of sugar. Allow this to boil, remove the scum as it rises, then run the whole through a sieve. Then cut a dozen pieces of bread, fry them in butter, & dry them in a cloth, shake some cinnamon & sugar over them, & simmer all slowly or put in an oven for 1/2 an hour. E.B. Ca—

Nicolas Appert spent many years working to develop a canning method for meat and fruit. His factories remained innovative but unprofitable, and he died a poor man in 1841 and was buried in a common grave. By then variants of his process were used to can foods ranging from New York oysters and Nantes sardines to Italian fruit and Pennsylvania tomatoes.

The availability of canned food played a crucial role in 19th century, feeding the enormous armies of the Crimean War, the U.S. Civil War and the Franco-Prussian War, and offering explorers and colonialists a taste of home in unfamiliar lands. Following the global depression of 1873, U.S. exports of canned foods boomed, led by the Campbell, Heinz and Borden companies.

A picture of Lincoln before the presidency.

Chicken Fricassee

MRS HALE'S NEW COOK BOOK
SARAH JOSEPHA HALE (1857)

> ### White Fricassee of Chicken.
>
> Draw and clean one pair of fowls, lay them in water for half an hour, then dry them and lay them in a stew-pan with milk and water, and a little salt, and let them simmer until cooked; put into a saucepan half a pint of cream, a quarter of a pound of butter, and a little grated nutmeg, stir this and set it on the fire to simmer, and stir in a wine glass of white wine; then lay in the cooked chicken, and let it remain in this, covered up, until dished. Chop up parsley and strew it over the chicken.

President Lincoln rarely enjoyed breakfast, and was said to have had an egg and biscuit on rare occasions. A simple lunch was in the offing, an apple with a glass of milk, and dinner could be entirely forgotten unless a tray of food was placed on him. "Abe can sit and think longer without food than any other person I have ever met," Lincoln's former law partner in Chicago wrote. And, shortly after his death, Lincoln's sister-in-law recalled, "He loved nothing and ate mechanically. I have seen him sit down at the table and never unless recalled to his senses, would he think of food."

Like all of us, Lincoln did have his comfort foods. He would eat most heartily and never lost a boyhood love of the familiar: Corn Dodgers, Kentucky Corn Cakes, Gooseberry Cobbler, Rail Splitters, and the favorite cookie of the time, Gingerbread. And it has been said that one of the few entrees that would tempt Lincoln was Chicken Fricassee. According to A Treasury of White House Cooking by Francois Rysavy, Lincoln "liked the chicken cut up in small pieces, fried with seasonings of nutmeg and mace and served with a gravy made of the chicken drippings." It was also said that when he grew exasperated with his cabinet, Mary Todd would order this to calm him down.

Destruction of a Rebel salt factory, on the coast of Florida, by the crew of the U.S. bark *Kingfisher*— sketched by an officer engaged

U.S. BARK 'KINGFISHER,' ST. JOSEPH'S BAY, FLA., Sept. 15, 1862.

"I am glad to say that, after waiting all this time, I have had a chance to see active service. You can imagine with what pleasure we received the order to up anchor, as we knew our destination was the salt-works, at the head of the bay."

"About two weeks since we had a lot of contrabands come off, who informed us that there were extensive salt-works at the town of St. Joseph, making from 100 to 150 bushels a day, and not yet completed. We sent a flag of truce, and politely informed them that they must stop, or we should destroy them. They paid no attention to us, but continued their fire day and night."

"We got under way at daylight, sailed up the bay with a fair wind, and came to anchor about a quarter of a mile from the works. As we came in sight we could perceive an unusual excitement, and observed wagons driving inland at a furious pace. We gave them two hours to quit, and then fired a few shells into the works, which had the effect of bringing two contrabands to the beach with a salt-bag, which they waved most furiously. We sent a boat for them, and found out that they had removed about two hundred bags of salt and some provisions, but that every thing remained with this exception; and also the intelligence that there were about eighty guerrillas, mounted, three miles back in the country, and would probably be down to see what was going on. As soon as we obtained this information we manned all the boats, leaving enough men on board to man the battery. I had been ordered to take command of the picket-guard, and station them about a quarter of a mile inland, surrounding the works. You may imagine that was rather skittish work with twenty men to go into the woods out of sight of the ship; but we all drew up on the beach, the pickets in front (in all about fifty men), loaded muskets and fixed bayonets—the whole under command of Mr. Hallet, executive officer. We started, whistling Yankee Doodle. I advanced my men in a straight line to the other side of the works, when we entered the woods and extended our lines entirely around the place. The main body then began their work of destruction, and in less than two hours the whole place was in flames, and the machinery broken up."

"I send you a sketch. The whole coast of Florida is lined with these works of a smaller size. This one, when finished, would have been capable of making five hundred bushels a day, at $10 per bushel. When the new military colony is fairly under way these salt factories will probably become of some national importance."

Excerpt from Harper's Weekly, November 15, 1862 on the destruction of a salt factory off the coast of Florida

Chili Pepper Sauce

*DIRECTIONS FOR COOKING BY THE TROOPS
BY FLORENCE NIGHTINGALE (1861)*

> **Chili Vinegar, or Essence.**
>
> Those who are fond of cayenne will find this far superior to the article sold as cayenne.
>
> Cut in half or pound fifty red English chilies, which can be purchased at the wholesale druggists;—it is a peculiar fine flavour. On the chilies pour a pint of the best wine vinegar or good brandy; put it into a bottle, cork tightly and let it stand fourteen days. A very little of this seasons delightfully, and is preferable to the deleterious substance sold as cayenne.

One of the more famous stories that the McIlhenny Company, manufacturers of the the ubiquitous TABASCO® brand of pepper sauce, has told concerns the origins of its peppers. Reportedly, a Confederate soldier, returning home from the war, traded the now famous tabasco peppers for a meal. The rest, they say, is history.

While this story may or may not be true, it is known that many condiments ranging from catsups to hot sauce were popular during the time of the war. One advantage that the McIlhenny Company can claim is the vast salt stores that were, and still are, underneath Avery Island, home of the company. Salt was a precious commidity for both soldiers and citizens, and these deposits were both jealously guarded and aggresively targeted in attacks to gain control of this resource.

A collection of antique bottles used for various TABASCO® brand products.

Blockade runners supplied items such as chocolate to the Southern ports. Many of the runners were painted gray to reduce visibility, the forerunner of the modern Navy's Haze Gray.

Chocolate Cake

HANDWRITTEN FAMILY RECIPE
CIVIL WAR ERA

Chocklate Cake
1 cup of sugar
butter the size of a [egg]
1 egg ½ cup butter milk
½ tea spoon soda
½ " " creäm tarter
2 cups of flour

Once considered food only for kings, chocolate made its way into ordinary life. However, unlike its most used form today as solid pieces or bars, early chocolate in the eighteenth and early nineteenth century was most frequently consumed as a beverage. By the civil war period, chocolate had made its way into many cooked goods as well as further variations of beverages. If you look at the Feeding America website for period cookbooks or you can find a period cookbook on google books, you can get recipes for using the chocolate. But, alas for true chocolate lovers, chocolate chip cookies (see the article "What No Chocolate Chip Cookies" in "Virginia's Veranda" to learn about cookies) were still unknown during the civil war period. Also, in researching recipes, sometimes a "chocolate cookie" or other chocolate baked good would not contain any chocolate. Instead, the item was intended to be eaten with a chocolate beverage.

Irish clam diggers, Boston, MA

Clam Soup

*DIRECTIONS FOR COOKING BY THE TROOPS
BY FLORENCE NIGHTINGALE (1861)*

> ### Clam Soup.
>
> Wash fifty of the small sand clams very clean. Put them into an iron pot, set it in a hot place and cover it up. When they become heated, the clams open; then take them from the shells. Put the clams aside in a pan, and pour the juice into a stew-pan; let it simmer for five minutes, strain it and rub two tablespoonfuls of butter and one of flour smoothly together; put the juice on to cook, and slowly add the flour and butter, stir it well together, add half a teaspoonful of salt, half of a nutmeg grated, and a pint of good cream; stir this well, let it simmer for ten minutes, chop up some parsley and throw in; then pour in the clams. One boil-up finishes, as the clams, like oysters, require very little cooking. If you use the large clams, they must be chopped.

"But when that smoking chowder came in, the mystery was delightfully explained. Oh! sweet friends, hearken to me. It was made of small juicy clams, scarcely bigger than hazel nuts, mixed with pounded ship biscuits and salted pork cut up into little flakes! the whole enriched with butter, and plentifully seasoned with pepper and salt.....we dispatched it with great expedition."

—Herman Melville 'Moby Dick

Clam soup, in the golden olden days, was a specialty food that was served at special occasion dinners, especially in the northern coastal states. 1820s New York saw booths set up in Central park featuring "baked beans, roast pig and punch, custards and clam soup" according to a local newspaper of the time. It was also an extravagance that some upper crust hotels such as the Flushing Hotel, also in New York, served.

Cod

*DIRECTIONS FOR COOKING BY THE TROOPS
BY FLORENCE NIGHTINGALE (1861)*

A Fresh Cod.

This is very nice. Clean it, and before putting it on the strainer rub it with salt, then lay it on the strainer, and cover it plentifully with cold water, and a tumbler full of vinegar; cook it as directed for other fish. An egg sauce must be served with this, which is made by chopping up three hard-boiled eggs, and stirring in well made drawn butter. Serve very hot. Garnish the fish with sprigs of parsley.

"How influential has the codfish been in the world's history? Wars have been fought over it, entire regional diets have been founded on it, the settlement of North America was based on it — and just recently a war nearly broke out on the high seas over it."

Barnes & Noble Book Review

Cod has been a vital source of food as well as oil for hundreds of years and was a major commodity swapped in the days of early international trading. For many in the coastal area of New England, a flaky well-cooked Cod was the Thanksgiving dinner of choice instead of the traditional turkey. Cod was also one of the staples of the Union army diet during the lean years of the war, providing various products for its soldiers in blue. This pressing and immediate need set up a fishing industry powerhouse along Massachusetts coastal regions during the

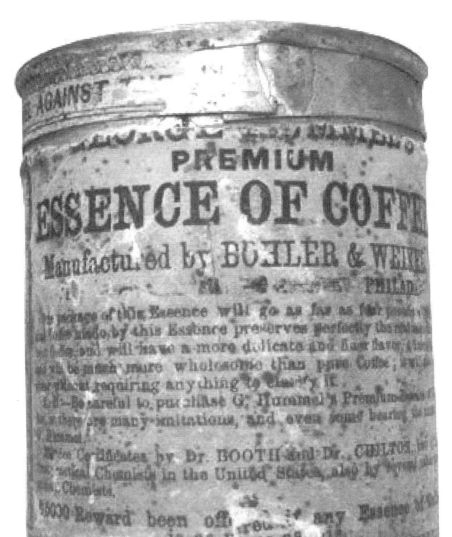

Coffee Syrup

*MRS. BEETON'S DICTIONARY OF EVERYDAY COOKERY
BY ISABELLA BEETON (1862)*

> **COFFEE SYRUP**
> [1862]
>
> This confection is exceedingly handy to travellers when proceeding on a long journey. Take half a pound of the best, roasted, ground coffee; boil the same in saucepan containing three quarts of water until the quantity is reduced to one quart; strain the latter off, and, when fined of all impurities, introduce the liquor into another clean saucepan, and let it boil over again, adding as much Lisbon sugar* to it as will constitute a thick syrup, like treacle; remove from the fire, and, when cold, pour it into bottles, corking the same tight down for use. Two teaspoonfuls of the syrup introduced into a moderate-sized teacup, and filled up with boiling water, will be fit for immediate use. If milk is at hand, use it *ad libitum*.

Readers may recognize this recipe as the precursor to instant coffee. Even in the midst of the Civil War, there was still one thing the North and South shared—a serious addiction to caffeine. In that respect, the Union clearly had an advantage. Not only did the North have more than two-thirds of the population and control most of the heavy industry, railroads, and financial reserves in the country, it hoarded supplies of the highly addictive little bean, leaving the Confederacy to wage its own war against java deprivation. Throughout the Civil War, coffee was as prevalent on the battlefields as it is in offices today. In fact, the Union army was fueled by the stuff to the point that, if there was no time to boil water, the Boys in Blue would chew on whole beans as they marched. And at night, Union campsites were dotted with tiny fires, each boiling a pot of coffee like a million miniature Starbucks.

Cedar Mountain, Virginia. Mrs. Hudson's house and cabbage patch beside the battlefield

Cold Slaw

MRS HALE'S NEW COOK BOOK
SARAH JOSEPHA HALE (1857)

Cold Slaw.

Select a white hard head of cabbage, cut it in half, and lay it in water for an hour; when ready, shave it with a cutter or sharp knife, very finely; put half a pint of vinegar on to boil, beat up the yolk of an egg with a little salt and cayenne, pour the boiling vinegar on the yolk, stir it well, and pour it over the shaved cabbage. This is nice with roast beef.

While this recipe terms it cold slaw, the common spelling is coleslaw and is derived from the Dutch term "koolsla" meaning cabbage salad. The British salad was termed cold slaw and it slowly became Americanized to coleslaw. Certainly a staple in the southern United States, this traditional BBQ side item has actually been around in one form or another since Roman times. It's gradually evolved from a cabbage salad that had vinegar as its only other ingredient to the mayonnaise based salad that began in the 1700s with the invention of mayonnaise. The sauce of cold slaw or coleslaw is often times served hot on this side dish, dependent on the chef's whim. While it currently a side item that is served with picnic items, during our ante-bellum days, it was a side dish that was served with fine foods such as roast beef, pork loin and other meat dishes.

President James Buchanan, the last president before the war, and seen by many as the worst for not stopping the hostilities.

Confederate Pudding

THE HOME MANUAL, OR, THE ECONOMICAL COOK AND HOUSE-BOOK. 5TH, ENLARGED BY ELIZABETH NICHOLSON (1865)

> Confederate Pudding : To one pint of flour add three eggs, half a teaspoonful of salæratus, one cup of molasses, and a half pound of dried peaches; cut fine. Sauce—a lump of butter about the size of a walnut; half a grated nutmeg; sweeten to taste, and as much brandy as you like, but don't get drunk; boil one hour.

If President James Buchanan uttered any memorable line during the Civil War era, it was doubtless the one he expressed to Abraham Lincoln on inauguration day, March 4, 1861. "My dear sir, if you are as happy in entering the White House as I shall feel on returning to Wheatland, you are a happy man indeed." Like many other retired presidents, Buchanan happily returned home, to renew acquaintance with friends and neighbors, and to focus on pleasant pursuits, less stressful than running a country in a turbulent era. One of our oldest presidents—nearing 70 upon his retirement—Buchanan actually left the White House in better physical shape than he entered it. This is not hard to appreciate, given his affliction in March of 1857 with what Roy F. Nichols has called "National Hotel disease." Over the course of the next month, Buchanan eased into a retirement regimen. He took quiet walks, examined the conditions of his estate, added staff, and kept in touch as best he could with former Cabinet officers, both about what had been done during the secession crisis under his watch, and what was now unfolding in Charleston Harbor. For much of the next four years, the War - "Buchanan's war," some called it - would dominate the news and ultimately reshape the meaning of American nationhood. Pennsylvania-born-and-bred Buchanan was no Confederate, but he did enjoy some of the rich and elegant desserts for which the South was justly famous. This was his favorite.

Cottage Cheese

CONFEDERATE RECEIPT BOOK
BY WEST AND JOHNSTON, RICHMOND (1863)

> COTTAGE CHEESE.—This is a good way of using up a pan of milk that is found to be turning sour. Having covered it, set it in a warm place till it becomes a curd, then pour off the liquid, and tie up the curd in a clean linen bag with a pointed end, and set a bowl under it to catch the droppings, but do not squeeze it. After it has drained ten or twelve hours transfer the curd to a deep dish, enrich it with some cream, and press and chop it with a large spoon till it is a soft mass, adding as you proceed an ounce or more of nice fresh butter.

The first known use of the term "cottage cheese" dates back to 1831 and is believed to have originated because the simple cheese was usually made in cottages from any milk left over after making butter. The curds and whey of nursery rhyme fame is another dish made from curds with whey, but it is uncertain what their consistency was, if they were drained at all or how they were curdled (which affects the flavor). Some writers claim they are equivalent or similar..

In America, the Pennsylvania Dutch were known for making their version of it, known as "schmear kase". One benefit then as now, is that the cottage cheese contained substantial amounts of protein, which was a precious commidty for both soldiers and the homefront.

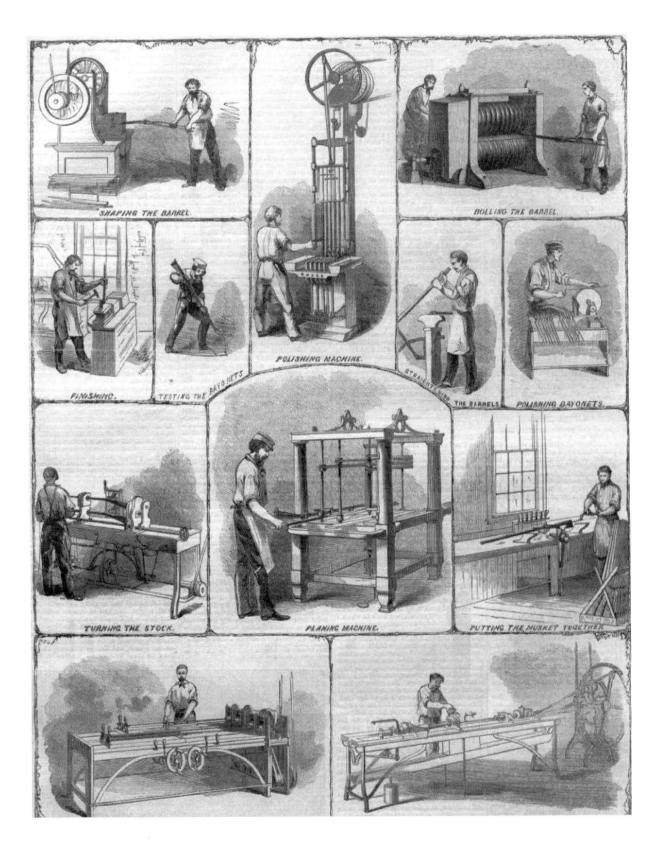

Crullers

*THE NATIONAL COOKBOOK BY
BOUVIER, PETERSON AND REED (1856)*

> **CRULLERS.**
>
> 400. Five eggs,
> Three-quarters of a pound of sugar,
> A quarter of a pound of butter,
> One table spoonful of ground cinnamon,
> Two table spoonsful of brandy,
> One table spoonful of salæratus,
> As much flour as will form a soft dough.
>
> Beat the butter and sugar together till it is light. Whisk the eggs, and then stir in the spice and liquor. Beat the whole very hard; add the salæratus, and as much flour as will form a soft dough, cut it in strips, twist them and drop them in a pot of boiling lard. When they are of a light brown they will be done. Sift sugar over them when cold.

The modern coffeebreak is a pale replica of an old institution. After finishing a difficult job, cabinetmakers in New York City sent out an apprentice who "speedily returned laden with wine, brandy, biscuits, and cheese." In shipyards in the same city, all work ceased several times a day as "every man and boy" in the yard was supplied with "cake or crullers, doughnuts, gingerbread, turnovers, a variety of sweet cookies," and liquid refreshments.

The American worker loved to drink, insisting that liquor be brought in during working hours. That a shipbuilder in Medford, Massachusetts, who refused his men "grog privileges" managed nevertheless to have work completed on a ship has been called a remarkable achievement. Philadelphia artisans insisted on their late afternoon drink, passing a jug around. Not that they abstained earlier. A journeyman there reported that "young apprentices learned to drink while they learned a trade." The youths made periodic trips to the local pub to fill the flasks journeymen brought with them to work. Before returning to the shop the apprentice would "rob the mail"--help himself to a drink and a sanck.

55

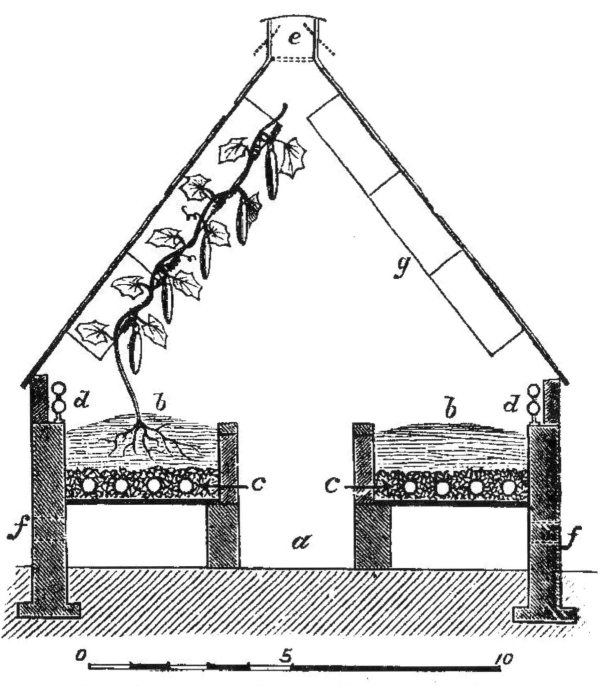

Fig. 14.—Span-Roofed Cucumber House.

Cucumbers

MRS. HALE'S NEW COOK BOOK
BY SARAH JOSEPHA HALE (1857)

CUCUMBERS.

To stew Cucumbers.—Pare eight or ten large cucumbers, and cut them into thick slices, flour them well, and fry them in butter; then put them into a sauce-pan with a tea-cupful of gravy; season it with Cayenne, salt and catsup. Let them stew for an hour, and serve them hot.

Many people today associate the cucumber, originally from India, with with array of pickles either home-canned or available in every corner grocery. One of the oldest vegetables in America, cucumbers were introduced by the Spanish to North America. However, given the spate of diseases that ravaged colonial times, there was a belief that only cooked vegetables were safe. In keeping with this, the cucumber earned a reputation for being "fit only for consumption by cows", leading to a moniker of "cowcumber".

According to Dr. William Kitchiner in 1829, "...the above recipe, rubbed through a tamis or fine sieve, will be entitled to be called 'cucumber sauce.' This is a very favorite sauce with lamb or mutton-cutlets, stewed rump-steaks, & c..." Consequently, the good doctor labeled an accompanying pickle recipe as "Vulgar Cucumbers", as it was not cooked, but merely soaked in a vinegar solution and not fit for proper society consumption.

Cure for Camp Itch

*CONFEDERATE RECEIPT BOOK
BY WEST AND JOHNSTON, RICHMOND (1863)*

> CURE FOR CAMP ITCH.—Take iodide of potassium, sixty grains, lard, two ounces, mix well, and after washing the body well with warm soap suds rub the ointment over the person three times a week. In seven or eight days the acarus or itch insect will be destroyed. In this recipe the horrible effects of the old sulphur ointment are obviated.

"Camp Itch" was a painful skin disease, involving itching, lesions, and inflammation, suffered by soldiers both North and South during the Civil War. Doctors debated the cause of the itch. Certainly some cases were really scabies, a very contagious skin disease caused by mites and quickly spread by shared blankets as well as in crowded conditions. Some doctors, however, stated that camp itch was not scabies as no "animaliculae" were present. Whether scabies or not, the itch resulted from the poor hygiene of troops who bathed infrequently, suffered numerous scratches and bites, and were generally very dirty. Then, when afflicted, the men scratched, making the problem worse. The itch became so severe in some cases that 31,947 Union troops and quite a number of Confederates had to be hospitalized for treatment of the infections that followed. The standard remedies were evidently sulphur and arsenic taken internally, plus external alkaline baths. Some doctors also prescribed a wash of sulphur and lime. Because many ingredients were difficult to get in the South, Confederate doctors sought to develop treatments using indigenous plants.

DELICIOUS BROWN BREAD

DIRECTIONS FOR COOKING BY THE TROOPS
BY FLORENCE NIGHTINGALE (1861)

> **DELICIOUS BROWN BREAD.**
>
> Take three pints of rye, and the same of corn meal of the best quality, a few tablespoonsful of mashed pumpkin, half a tea cup of molasses, two teaspoonsful of salt, a teaspoonful of soda dissolved in warm water, and half a cup of yeast; mix all with warm water, make it as stiff as can be conveniently stirred with the hand, grease two earthen or iron pans which are preferable, put the bread in them, have a bowl of cold water at hand, to smooth over the top, dipping your hand into the water; it rises faster than other bread, and, therefore should not be made over night in summer, and in winter should stand in a cool place, until after the fire is in the oven. It requires a hot oven, and long baking—at least four hours.

"For it is we who must pray for our daily bread, and if He grants it to us, it is only through our labour, our skill and preparation."

— Paracelsus

Because the requisite hardtack that the common solider received was just that, hard, many soldiers set out to duplicate the delicious brown rye breads of home, if they had the ingredients available to them. But in most cases, they simply wrote home asking for the memorable foods to be sent to them. Unfortunately, those at home usually didn't have that much more to eat than the soldiers asking for the foods. Moreover, sending care packages out to their loved ones often didn't result in success as people were starving all over and packages were stolen in transit, many never making it to their intended destination.

DELMONICO'S.
BEAVER AND WILLIAM STREETS, OPPOSITE THE COTTON EXCHANGE.

Delmonico's Chocolate Pudding

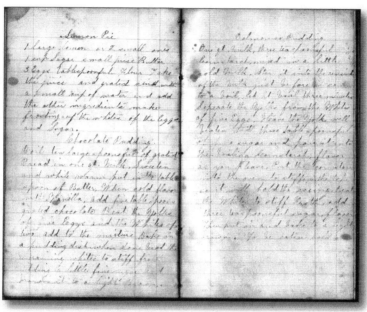

Delmonico's is the name of series of restaurants of varying duration, quality, and fame located in New York City. The original and most famous was operated by the Delmonico family during the 19th and early 20th centuries, closing due to a Prohibition-era slowdown in 1923. The original Delmonico's began in a rented pastry shop at 23 William Street in 1827, appearing listed as a restaurant in 1830. Relocating several times before settling at 2 South William Street for eighty years, it is credited with being the first restaurant in America to allow patrons to order from a menu à la carte, as opposed to table d'hôte. It is also claimed to be the first to employ a separate wine list.

As the decades passed this Delmonico's reputation spread, being widely regarded as one of the nation's top fine dining establishments and birthplace of the universally imitated Delmonico steak. At the peak of "Delmonico's" fame the family operated four restaurants under the name simultaneously, and a total of ten during their tenure. The above recipe is for the their famed Chocolate pudding of the time.

Woven eel bucks to be lowered into the river.

Eel Soup

DIRECTIONS FOR COOKING BY THE TROOPS
BY FLORENCE NIGHTINGALE (1861)

Eel Soup.

Take two good sized onions, peel, wash and slice them, and put them into the soup pot; put a lump of butter in and brown them. Have ready cleaned and washed five or six good sized eels, cut them into pieces and pour on them three quarts of boiling water; remove all the scum; when the pot begins to boil, tie in a bundle some thyme, summer savoury and parsley, and also add half a teaspoonful of allspice and the same of pepper corns and salt. Cover this tightly and let it boil slowly for two hours; then strain it carefully. Have ready, in a stew-pan, some thickening—two spoonsful of butter melted in the pan and flour dredged in to a paste—on this pour the soup, and let it simmer ten minutes. While it is simmering, fry some pieces of eels a nice brown and lay in a tureen; on these pour the soup. Serve very hot.

Another gift from the German immigrants was the eel soup. The soup name is derived from the words "all soup" and originally contained no eel at all. It simply had had ham bones that were left over along with extra vegetables that had yet to be discarded or eaten. To those not familiar with the term all soup or "aol suppe" it sounded like eel and everyone always wondered where the eel was in the soup. Enterprising innkeepers in Hamburg, Germany decided to capitalize on the mystery, added the long eel into the soups and started doubling the price. So was born the eel soup that now had eel as an ingredient. The recipe has evolved and now it has a multitude of different recipes all claiming to be the original.

Winemakers in a field, 1849

Elder Wine

GODEY'S LADY'S BOOK
BY LOUIS A. GODEY (1860)

> ### Elder Wine.
>
> Put to six gallons and a half of ripe elder berry juice, twenty-two pounds of brown sugar, and nineteen gallons of water; in this water before adding it, boil three ounces of ginger, four ounces of alspice and one ounce of cloves, let it boil until a fine aromatic flavor is imparted to the water; then strain it through a cloth, and add it to the juice; a small quantity of the water can be flavored, it is not necessary to boil the whole; when almost cold add half a pint of good brewer's yeast; let it ferment fourteen days in a clean cask, then bung it up closely; in six months bottle it, and in each bottle put five or six blanched bitter almonds; it is fit for use as soon as bottled, and is a wholesome beverage.

Sometimes called Elderberry wine, this wine is said to come from a long line of healing potions. In fact, the Egyptians were known to take the flowers of the elderberry plant and use them for the healing of burns, much like what is done with an Aloe plant today. Additionally, when the British began making elderberry wine in the 1600s, they claimed it was a cure for the cold and could also extend your life. Even today, there are stories that suggest a glass or two of elderberry wine can rid you of flu symptoms and keep the cold at bay. When making elderberry wine, some winemakers choose to let it mellow an extra couple of months turning the wine into brandy, but that's a personal choice.

"SHROVETIDE: TOSSING THE PANCAKE." BY A. HUNT.

Flannel Cake

MRS HALE'S NEW COOK BOOK
SARAH JOSEPHA HALE (1857)

Flannel Cakes.

One quart of new milk, thickened with flour to the consistency of fritter batter, one tablespoonful of butter, two eggs well beaten, one large spoonful of yeast, and a little salt. Mix this all well together; set it to rise at night for breakfast. They must not be stirred in the morning. Bake on the griddle, as buckwheat cakes.

As seen with many recipes of the Civil War era, specific directions are often times not given as they are in recipes today. The recipes of old assume your expertise in the kitchen. For example, this recipe assumes that you know what consistency fritter batter would be. It also assumes you will know why not to stir them in the morning. In actuality, flannel cakes are thin pancakes, much like a crepe. You wouldn't want to stir it in the morning because you want the batter to remain thick enough to cook in a small round pan without running. If you have no experience cooking these types of items in the past, you wouldn't know the whys and wherefores of the recipe by reading it, you'd simply have to trust the writer of the recipe on the issue. Flannel cakes originated from the Pennsylvania Dutch, and were supposedly named for Dutch word for "molten" batter.

Fruitcake

*HANDWRITTEN FAMILY RECIPE
CIVIL WAR ERA*

The fruitcake is an often-maligned Christmas treat. Some people love them, while others have made fruitcakes the objects of every sort of holiday joke. People who enjoy fruitcakes are sometimes considered so crazy by the general population that they've even been dubbed fruitcakes. So what is a fruitcake? It is a heavy cake full of fruit, and nuts, held together with a little heavy cake or bread and lots of sugar and alcohol. This special holiday cake is also one of the most labor intensive items you can run across often taking months to make. According to Et Tu, Fruitcake, food scholars date fruitcake back to ancient Egypt and the Roman Empire. According to some historians, Egyptian fruitcake was considered an essential food for the afterlife and there are those today who maintain that this is the only thing they are good for. In ancient Rome, raisins, pine nuts and pomegranate seeds were added to barley mash, making the fruitcake not only handy and lethal catapult ammunition, but also hearty compact foodstuff for the long campaigns waged by the conquering Roman legions. The fruitcake as we know it seems to have hit it's peak of popularity and taken it's heavy form in Victorian England, where it became a staple of high tea.

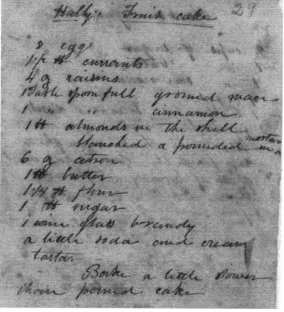

Gherkins

HANDWRITTEN FAMILY RECIPE
CIVIL WAR ERA

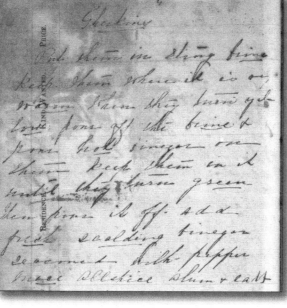

In 1869, Mary H. Hill of Nelson County, VA, somehow got her hands on a salesman's sample book and proceeded to use it as a scrapbook for her favorite recipes over the next decade or so. What makes her book stand out is its non-categorical nature. The volume has newspaper clippings of recipes pasted on some pages. Other pages feature handwritten recipes. And the book itself is a repurposed salesman's sample book. So we could label this book a scrapbook, a cookbook, a salesman's sample book, or a bit of all three! Mary included some great recipes found in newspapers, as well as household recipes for items such as bleach and dyes. Her handwritten recipes include how to prepare an East India pickle, or gherkin, apple custard, and tip top cakes. Finally, at the end of the volume, Mary pasted a newspaper clipping about the unveiling of the Stonewall Jackson statue in Virginia.

GINGERBREAD

HANDWRITTEN FAMILY RECIPE
CIVIL WAR ERA

Although gingerbread has been traditionally associated with happy times and festive occasions, it was not specific to the celebration of Christmas. For example, before the Civil War, in New England, the first Tuesday of every June (Muster Day) all men from 18 to 45 were required to go to military training. Many of them would take their families. The families would stay in the tents with their men at night and gather around the training fields during the day, sitting on the grass with their children as if they were simply having an all-day picnic. It became a festive occasion which included gingerbread as an essential part of the tradition. Women and children attended Muster Day with their loved ones and supported them in their military training.

75

Green Corn Pudding

MRS HALE'S NEW COOK BOOK
SARAH JOSEPHA HALE (1857)

> ### Green Corn Pudding.
>
> Take two quarts of grated corn, one quarter of a pound of butter, one pint of milk, two eggs, and one table-spoonful of flour; salt to your taste; beat these well together. Bake it three quarters of an hour in a slow oven.

If you were having folks over for dinner, the big afternoon meal enjoyed in the south, one might serve green corn pudding as it was seen as a "company" dish. This rich dish wasn't actually green. The title was given to the dish not because the recipe called for under-ripened corn, but just the opposite. During the 1800s, fresh corn was often referred to as "green" corn. The fresher and juicier the corn in this recipe, the better the results. In the 1800s, there was no distinction, as there is today, between sweet corn that we eat and the field corn that goes to animals. It was all just corn. When cooking this dish, make sure that your oven is not too hot as you don't want your pudding to curdle.

Hair Tonic

HANDWRITTEN FAMILY RECIPE
CIVIL WAR ERA

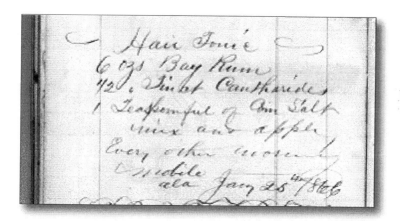

One way the quintessential southern gentleman kept his dashing good looks was with the application of hair tonics with Bay Rum as one of its main ingredients. While men and women could buy tonics from the store in the 1800s, many people still cooked up their own concoctions. One of the biggest draws of the tonic is its lack of oiliness and the lightweight feel on the hair. Additionally, it stimulates blood flow within the scalp. When using, keep in mind it takes very little of this homemade product to produce results and a batch will last you a while. If making up today, you may want to bottle it and give as gifts as the yield is impressive. This product can be bottled in a tap out version or put in a spray-type bottle for use after showering.

Ham n' Chicken Pie

GODEY'S LADY'S BOOK
BY LOUIS A. GODEY (1860)

Ham and Chicken Pie.

Cut some thin slices of cold cooked ham, lay them in the bottom of a dish, and cut a cold boiled fowl up as for a fricasse; lay one half of the fowl on the ham, and season with a very little pepper and salt, and a little grated nutmeg. Rub the hard boiled yolks of two eggs, a spoonful of flour, and a large spoonful of butter, and stir this into half a pint of any nice broth, then pour this over the chicken, then another layer of thin slices of ham, and then the remainder of the chicken; then pour on a little more broth, and cover the whole with a nice paste, and bake it slowly half an hour. Serve hot.

In the years prior to the Civil War, food was plentiful and the culinary masterpieces of deliciousness prepared in southern kitchens were a wonder to behold. Ham and chicken pies were another example of extravagance and dishes that were made for special occasions like Christmas, Easter or New Years Day dinner. Weddings were another time when the stops were pulled and rich tasty dishes full of two meats, rich creams and eggs were served in bulk. With the rationing of the war, dishes such as this would have been a luxury if the ingredients were available at all. After the war, it took years for livestock and gardens that had been depleted or left un-cared for to get back to the glory of pre-war days.

Hogs on farm, North Carolina.

How to Cook Pig's Head

GODEY'S LADY'S BOOK
BY LOUIS A. GODEY (1860)

How to Cook Pig's Head.

Have ready cleaned the head, feet, and haslet, put them on to boil with plenty of cold water, and a teaspoonful of salt, reserving the liver to cook separately. Let it boil slowly for two hours, skimming it carefully; then take the head and haslet from the water, take out every bone carefully, put the head into a baking dish, sprinkle over it some finely powdered sage, a little cayenne, grate the rind of a lemon, and cover

---

"This head is for the beast. It's a gift."
— William Golding, Lord of the Flies

The culinary dish Pig's Head goes by many names from the British contribution of "Brawn" to the brasher American version of "Head Cheese". But the fact remains that this inexpensive cut of pork is one that attracts attention whenever it's fixed or featured. When dining on this Irish born delicacy, invite family and friends to help you out, as a full head could easily feed six people at a sitting. If you're planning to cook for less, you can always order a half-head, but have the butcher do the sawing for you. Additionally, you'll want your butcher to "prepare" the head ahead of time as shaving your food before eating is not always something one will want to do. Part of what makes this cut of meet good is the excess fat and juicy skin. You'll find the best parts of the pig's head are the cheek, the tongue and under the eyes.

Rare photo of Robert E. Lee's slaves Selina Gray, personal maid to Robert's wife Mary Anna, and her children

Indian Loaf

*DIRECTIONS FOR COOKING BY THE TROOPS
BY FLORENCE NIGHTINGALE (1861)*

> **INDIAN LOAF.**
>
> To one quart of skimmed sweet milk, put one teacup of molasses, one teaspoonful of soda dissolved in a cup of new milk, a pint of corn meal, a large handful of flour, and a little salt; this must be well beaten, then pour it into pans to bake, which requires five hours. Serve hot, and mixed just as baked.

Like so many recipes that were popular during the Civil War, molasses was a commonly listed ingredient. It's not that people of the era didn't like sugar, but it was much harder to come by so molasses would be substituted. Sugar was designated a "luxury item" by the Confederate government, especially in non-sugar producing states. Blockades by the northern ships also prevented the importing of sugar from Louisiana, Florida and the Caribbean to North and South Carolina as well as Virginia. Unfortunately, in the later years of the Civil War, even molasses was hard to come by. Because dessert items were far and few between on the marching trail, men would often take to sweetening breads in an effort to bake something pleasant or different for a change. This recipe, however, took 5 hours to cook and would have only have been used during down time or slow winter months.

Italian Syrup

HANDWRITTEN FAMILY RECIPE
CIVIL WAR ERA

Italian involvement in the Civil War was intense and passionate. Their militant hero back home, Giuseppe Garibaldi, was their inspiration; his republican views led many Italians to back the Union cause, though they were represented in the Southern armies as well. Their stories are fascinating and colorful. Count Luigi Palma di Cesnola, a veteran of the Crimean War, established a military academy in New York City, where many young Italians learned the art of war and later served in the Union army. Cesnola, for instance, was left wounded and pinned under his horse after fighting JEB Stuart's cavalry at Aldie, Virginia, in June 1863; while a prisoner of war, he agitated for better treatment for prisoners, to the point that his captors put him in charge of the prison commissary at Belle Isle. The above is an Italian recipe for syrup from the 1860's.

The original candy store that would become the now-famous Jelly Belly company. Founded by Gustav Goelitz.

Jelly Beans

*HANDWRITTEN FAMILY RECIPE
CIVIL WAR ERA*

The great-great jelly bean ancestor first appeared in the 1800s, but jelly candies of one kind or another have been around for thousands of years. "Turkish delight," a citrus, honey and rose water jell, has been putting smiles on kids' faces since biblical times.

Fast forward 2500 years. When the penny candy craze came along in America during the 1800's, candy makers began experimenting with tricky sugar candies. The jelly candy inspired by Turkish delight was shaped into a bean and given a soft shell using a French process called "panning". The first jelly bean was created by an American candymaker whose name has since been lost in time, but it was probably early in the 1800s. An 1861 advertisement recommended sending jelly beans to soldiers fighting in the Civil War.

General Jubal Early never did surrender, incidentally; he escaped to Mexico instead, dressed up as a "farmer."

Jubal Early Punch

HANDWRITTEN FAMILY RECIPE
CIVIL WAR ERA

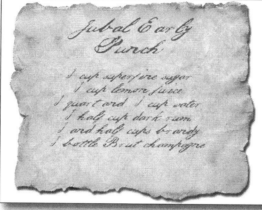

What, no bourbon? You'd imagine a punch named after a Confederate general would have at least a little of the stuff in it. We've got a theory. (Don't we always?) Jubal Anderson Early was a gentleman of the antebellum South, and true southern gentlemen generally left whiskey for Yankees and other representatives of the classless society. Instead, they drank imported. The war changed all that, of course -- all the Rhett Butlers in the world couldn't have run enough champagne and port and brandy and good old Jamaican rum past the Union blockade to keep the rebel gentry properly lubricated (not that they imbibed any more than their northern counterparts). Corn whiskey is what they had, and corn whiskey is what they drank.

Still, we can easily picture Old Jube -- a man known to tipple, mind you -- rudely pushing aside the proffered cup of corn, most likely with a curse. "I was never blessed with popular or captivating manners," he wrote in his memoirs, "and the consequence was that I was often misjudged and thought to be haughty and disdainful in my temperament." Nothing personal, in other words. Matter of principle, and you don't bend on principles.

Kisses

GODEY'S LADY'S BOOK
BY LOUIS A. GODEY (1860)

> **KISSES.**
>
> To six whites of eggs, one pound finest powdered sugar. Beat the eggs to a solid froth, and add the sugar by degrees, adding at times the juice of one lemon, and a very few drops oil of lemon. Before all the sugar is mixed, try one in the oven on a piece of paper. If frothy and soft to the touch, they require more sugar, but be sure not to add too much, or they will be hard and creamy. Bake in a tolerably quick oven, dropped on paper.

One thing that the cook of today will notice immediately with the recipes of the Civil War era do not have temperatures on the baking instructions. They did not have a thermostat dial to set an oven to and pre-heating was a waste of firewood. Instead, the instructions, as in this Kisses recipe, state to cook in a slow, moderate or quick oven. What does this mean to the modern chef? A very slow oven can be assumed to be set at 300-325, a slow oven to 325-350, a moderate oven to 350-375 and a quick oven to 400-425. These are approximate temperatures that are liable to be off by 25 degrees in either direction as what may have been fast to one cook was merely moderate to another.

Lady Baltimore Cake

HANDWRITTEN FAMILY RECIPE
CIVIL WAR ERA

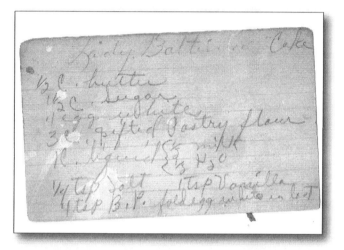

"I should like a slice, if you please, of Lady Baltimore," I said with extreme formality. I returned to the table and she brought me the cake, and I had my first felicitous meeting with Lady Baltimore. Oh, my goodness! Did you ever taste it? It's all soft, and it's in layers, and it has nuts — but I can't write any more about it; my mouth waters too much. Delighted surprise caused me once more to speak aloud, and with my mouth full, "But, dear me, this is delicious!"

—Owen Wister

These were the words written in description of a cake not yet invented. Wister was a popular romance novelist of the era and his novel *Lady Baltimore* sent the country in search of a southern delight that came entirely from his imagination. Naturally, recipes began to pop up everywhere and a southern classic wedding cake was born.

U.S. Sanitary Commission, dispensing supplies to officers

Lemonade

*DIRECTIONS FOR COOKING BY THE TROOPS
BY FLORENCE NIGHTINGALE (1861)*

> **CITRIC ACID LEMONADE.**
>
> Dissolve 1 oz. citric acid in one pint of cold water; add 1 lb. 9 oz. white sugar; mix well to form a thick syrup; then put in 19 pints cold water, slowly mixing well.

Lemonade was not just for enjoyment on a hot's summer's day; it was also considered to be medicinal to treat the slew a slew of ailments. Sailors as well had used lemons and lemonade, mixed with rum of course, for years to treat scurvy. Reports have lingered of General "Stonewall" Jackson always being in possession of lemons, eating them whole to ease his dyspepsia. Whether accurate or not, Jackson had a love of all fruits, an affinity he developed whilst serving in Mexico.

In 1863 Jane Swisshelm visited Campbell Hospital in Washington. She wrote about the experience in her autobiography, Half a Century (1880), where she was aghast at conditions in a Washington hospital. As a result, she took an ad out in the *New York Tribune*:

"Hospital gangrene has broken out in Washington, and we want lemons! lemons! lemons! lemons! No man or woman in health, has a right to a glass of lemonade until these men have all they need; send us lemons!"

Post-Civil War Easter Egg Hunt at the White House

Loaf Cake Without Eggs

GODEY'S LADY'S BOOK
BY LOUIS A. GODEY (1860)

> **LOAF CAKE WITHOUT EGGS.**
>
> Three pounds of flour, one and a half pounds sugar, one and a half pounds butter, one and a half pounds raisins, one nutmeg, one tablespoonful cinnamon, two gills wine, one half pint yeast, one pint milk; put the milk, butter and yeast into the flour and let it rise.

Throughout history, cooks have known what texture and shape eggs bring to cakes. But during war and depressed times, eggs and sugar both are rationed and hard to come by. That's where the ingenuity of chefs all over the world step up and a new recipe is born. Like many other recipes of similar design, the loaf cake without eggs relies on the raisins to provide the sweetness. Boiling the raisins with sugar and spices creates syrup that can often times even replace the butter in the recipe. Other names for this cake include Civil War Cake, Boiled Raisin Cake and Eggless, Milkless, Butterless Cake. The various versions of the cake resurfaced again during America's Great Depression of the 1930s and again during the hard rationed days on the home front of WWII.

New England Lobsterman

Lobster Salad

MRS. BEETON'S DICTIONARY OF EVERYDAY COOKERY
BY ISABELLA BEETON (1865)

LOBSTER SALAD.

Extract the fish from the shell, place it in the centre of the dish in which it is to be served, in the form of a pyramid; arrange the salad round tastefully, and add salad mixture. This dish is not infrequently garnished with the smallest claws of the fish. This is a matter of fancy—or thus: The first row is formed of cut cucumbers, the second of eggs boiled hard, and each egg split into four pieces, and the points laid round the salad; the third and bottom row is composed of slices of beets and lobsters, garnished with parsley.

"A woman should never be seen eating or drinking, unless it be lobster salad and Champagne, the only true feminine and becoming viands."

— Lord Byron

No fine wedding dinner would have been complete without an ornate lobster salad on the table. While of course there was no single typical fare for any Civil War wedding, lobster salad was as common as cheese straws or chocolate fountain might be today. Social and financial considerations also dictated the menu as well as the distance from a coastal area where lobster was in ready supply. The main difference you'll find from this lobster salad and one of today is the lack of mayonnaise in the recipe. That luxury did not come into commercial use until the early 1900s. Considering how long wedding dinners lasted back in the 1800s though, the lack of mayonnaise in products is probably the best as it would have forced foods to go "bad" much quicker.

Macaroni

MRS HALE'S NEW COOK BOOK
SARAH JOSEPHA HALE (1857)

> *To dress Macaroni.*—Wash and drain as much macaroni as you desire for dinner; put it on to boil in tepid water. When it is soft enough to pass a fork through, take it off, drain it through a cullender, wipe out the skillet, and return it immediately back again. Then add milk enough to half cover it, salt and red pepper to your taste, a piece of butter as large as a turkey's egg, and grated cheese as plentifully as you please; stew it all together, while stirring it for 5 or 10 minutes; then throw it out into a dish, cover the top with grated bread crumbs and set it in the oven for a few minutes to brown on the top. If left long in the oven it will dry up and become tough and unpalatable.

While Macaroni Cheese, as the British call it, has been a popular dish in England since the Victorian era, it's only been widely eaten in America since just after the Civil War. Due to the existence of only a few pasta factories in America, the noodles were not widely distributed and only wealthy families could afford to buy it prior to then. Americans can trace back the beginnings of macaroni and cheese in America to Thomas Jefferson. While he may not have been the first to bring the arc-shaped noodle across the pond, he did own a pasta maker as early as 1793 and it's been recorded that he served macaroni pie at the White House in 1802. Furthermore, records show he continued to purchase the pasta after his tenure as president.

Macaroni

MRS HALE'S NEW COOK BOOK
SARAH JOSEPHA HALE (1857)

> *To dress Macaroni.*—Wash and drain as much macaroni as you desire for dinner; put it on to boil in tepid water. When it is soft enough to pass a fork through, take it off, drain it through a cullender, wipe out the skillet, and return it immediately back again. Then add milk enough to half cover it, salt and red pepper to your taste, a piece of butter as large as a turkey's egg, and grated cheese as plentifully as you please; stew it all together, while stirring it for 5 or 10 minutes; then throw it out into a dish, cover the top with grated bread crumbs and set it in the oven for a few minutes to brown on the top. If left long in the oven it will dry up and become tough and unpalatable.

While Macaroni Cheese, as the British call it, has been a popular dish in England since the Victorian era, it's only been widely eaten in America since just after the Civil War. Due to the existence of only a few pasta factories in America, the noodles were not widely distributed and only wealthy families could afford to buy it prior to then. Americans can trace back the beginnings of macaroni and cheese in America to Thomas Jefferson. While he may not have been the first to bring the arc-shaped noodle across the pond, he did own a pasta maker as early as 1793 and it's been recorded that he served macaroni pie at the White House in 1802. Furthermore, records show he continued to purchase the pasta after his tenure as president.

Malina Pie

MRS HALE'S NEW COOK BOOK
SARAH JOSEPHA HALE (1857)

MALINA PIE.

Take cold mutton or veal, chop it very finely; then to one pint of minced meat, stir in the yolks of four well beaten eggs, the juice of one lemon, and the rind thinly grated, two small onions very finely chopped, half of a grated nutmeg, two large spoonsful of mushroom catsup, a very little cayenne, and salt to the taste. Mix this well together, and cut up into very small pieces a half quarter of a pound of butter and stir through it, then line a dish with good paste, and put this in to bake until it is a nice brown. Serve with a nice gravy made of the bones of the cold meats

A meat-filled pie is certainly not a new idea as European medieval pies were very popular. But those tasty pies usually had a variety of stuffings whereas the single ingredient pie such as mutton or veal pie did not come into existence until the colonists came to North America in the 1600s. Pies were a popular dish to make because your precious ingredients would last longer as a piecrust required less flour than a loaf of bread. Foods that had been stored over the winter could be used in the savory pies and topped with potatoes in the case of a shepherd's pie or mutton pie. The Shepherd's pie originated in the UK where there were plenty of sheep although variations include cottage pie, which is made with beef instead.

Maryland Biscuits

MRS HALE'S NEW COOK BOOK
SARAH JOSEPHA HALE (1857)

> **Maryland Biscuit.**
>
> Take any quantity of flour you think the size of the family may require; put in salt, and a lump or table-spoonful of good lard to a half pound of flour—rub it well in the flour; then moisten it with new milk, work it well, and beat it with a rolling-pin until perfectly light. On the lightness depends the goodness of the biscuit. Bake rather slowly, a light brown.

The famous biscuits of the southern Atlantic state of Maryland got it's start up in the southern and eastern shore back during the antebellum hey day. Because of the lack of leavening, this technique of making bread and leaving it to rise was one of the only ways possible. It stems from the Indian process of beating corn for cooking and consists of lard salt, flour and water. Like the corn of the Indians, it has to be beaten in some way. In the beginning, one took all the ingredients and mixed them together by hand before placing them on a smooth wood block or stump. The servants or the cook of the family would then beat the dough with a special mallet that was used only for biscuits. Beating the dough would trap the air inside the dough and then one could shape the biscuits by hand and knead it with your fingers to get the desired look.

Medicines

HANDWRITTEN FAMILY RECIPE
CIVIL WAR ERA

Eli Lilly was an American soldier, pharmaceutical chemist, industrialist, entrepreneur, and founder of the Eli Lilly and Company pharmaceutical corporation. Lilly enlisted in the Union Army during the American Civil War; he recruited a company of men to serve with him in an artillery battery, was later promoted to colonel, and was given command of a cavalry unit. He was captured near the end of the war and held as a prisoner of war until its conclusion. After the war, he attempted to run a plantation in Mississippi, but failed and returned to his pharmacy profession after the death of his wife. Lilly remarried and worked in several pharmacies with partners before opening his own business in 1876 with plans to manufacture drugs and market them wholesale to pharmacies. His company became successful and is still in operation today.

PLANET

VIRGINIA'S UNRIVALLED
RACE HORSE

This renowned Racer and Stallion will make his season of 1866, at BULLFIELD, the farm of Major THOMAS DOSWELL, in the county of HANOVER, twenty-four miles above Richmond, commencing March 1st, and ending July 15th, at $50 the season, with $2 to the groom.

Special attention will be given to the care and management of Mares sent to him, but in no event will be responsible for accidents.

They shall be fed with grain at 50 cents per diem.

All charges must be paid before the Mares are taken away.

THOMAS & THOMAS W. DOSWELL.

Mint Julep

GODEY'S LADY'S BOOK
BY LOUIS A. GODEY (1860)

> For the receipt-book let the following be copied:—First, *Cocktail* is composed of water, with the addition of rum, gin, or brandy, as one chooses—a third of the spirit to two-thirds of the water; add bitters, and *enrich* with sugar and nutmeg: in *sling*, the bitters are omitted.—Second, *Mint Julep*. Put four or five stalks of unbruised mint into a tumbler, on them place a lump of ice; add brandy, water, and sugar.—Third, *Apple-toddy*, says Mr. Willard, the bar-keeper of the City Hotel, who never forgets the face of a customer, is thus made: Have the fairest apples rolled in brown paper, which wet with water, and then bury them in live embers till they are thoroughly roasted and quite soft; then a fourth part of apples, a fourth part of brandy, a fourth part of water, a lump of ice, and the whole to be *rich* with a fourth part of sugar, makes the agreeable compound. N. B. If there is no nutmeg convenient, a scrape or two of the mudler (wooden sugar-breaker) will answer the purpose.

"I saw here for the first time a hailstorm, that is to say, a mint julep made with a hailstorm around it. The drink is manufactured pretty much as usual and well filled with a quantity of ice chopped in small pieces, which is then put in the shape of a fillet around the outside of the tumbler where it adheres like a ring of rock candy and forms an external icy application to your lower lip as you drink it, while the ice within the glass presses against your upper lip. It is nectar, they say, in this part of the country."

No drink or food either, for that matter, conjures up the wistful bygone days of the pre-Civil War south more than the Mint Julep.

Molasses Cookies

HANDWRITTEN FAMILY RECIPE
CIVIL WAR ERA

Molasses Cookies
3 cups molasses — or 2C. molasses & 1C. sugar
1½ " lard
4 tsp. soda dissolved in scant cup water
1 tsp cinnamon
1 tsp ginger
flour enough to thicken

General Robert E. Lee was a career military officer who is best known for having commanded the Confederate Army of Northern Virginia in the American Civil War. The son of Revolutionary War officer Henry "Light Horse Harry" Lee III and a top graduate of the United States Military Academy, Robert E. Lee distinguished himself as an exceptional officer and combat engineer in the United States Army for 32 years. When Virginia declared its secession from the Union in April 1861, Lee chose to follow his home state, despite his personal desire for the Union to stay intact and despite the fact that President Abraham Lincoln had offered Lee command of the Union Army. Lee would ultimately surrender to Grant at Appomattox Court House on April 9, 1865. By this time, Lee had been promoted to the commanding officer of all Confederate forces. This recipe came from Stradford Hall, Virginia, Lee's birthplace. It is said to be a favorite cookie of the Lee family, especially Robert E. Lee. The cookies are baked at the Lee plantation and served with warm cider to visitors.

New Orleans Gumbo

MISS LESLIE'S COMPLETE COOKERY. DIRECTIONS FOR COOKERY.
BY ELIZA LESLIE: 1858

New Orleans Gumbo.

Take a good sized pair of chickens, and cut them as for a fricassee; flour them well and put them into a pan with a good sized piece of butter, and fry them a nice brown; then lay them in a soup pot and pour on three quarts of hot water, let them simmer slowly two hours; then rub some flour and butter together for a thickening, and stir in a little cayenne and salt. Strain fifty oysters, and pour the juice into the soup. Just before serving, stir into the soup two large spoonsful of finely powdered sassafras leaves; let this simmer five minutes, and then add the oysters. Have ready some rice boiled dry, and garnish the chicken, which can be taken out of the gumbo, and makes a nice dish. Serve all hot.

"The great dish of New Orleans, and which it claims having the honor of invented, is the gumbo. There is no dish which at the same time so tickles the palate, satisfies the appetite, furnished the body with nutriment sufficient to carry on the physical requirements, and costs so little as a Creole Gumbo. It is a dinner in itself, being soup, piece de résistance, entremet and vegetable in one. Healthy, and not heating to the stomach and easy of digestion, it should grace every table."

William H. Coleman

This thick, dark soup mixes rice, vegetables and a meat or seafood together, as a start. But like so many great recipes, the one constant is the evolving nature of the recipe. The only rules that seem to stay are that it has to have rice and it should be thickened with something. While most people use a roux today, that was less common in the 19th century recipes. Still others use an okra or file' powder. But, you have been warned. One should never use both, as this is considered extremely uncultured.

THE GREEN-EYED MONSTER.
Tomkins calls early on his Intended, in order to have a pleasant little visit Alone, with the above Success.

New Years Cookies

HANDWRITTEN FAMILY RECIPE
CIVIL WAR ERA

While normally New Year's Day is a day of celebrating, fine foods and camaraderie, New Years Day of 1861 was not your typical holiday in neither the south, nor the north. South Carolina had only recently seceded from the Union on December 20, 1860 and there was a great deal of anxiety of the election of Abraham Lincoln the previous November. Talk of war was everywhere and newspapers of the day carried recruitment announcements for both the Army and the Navy. The president of the United States, James Buchanan requested a day of fasting and prayer for January 4th and churches all over the north were making plans to help host it. Preparations for war were being made with lots of excitement, pomp and circumstance, neither side knowing exactly how long or how hard the battle would be.

Okra Soup

*EVERY-DAY THINGS; OR, USEFUL KNOWLEDGE
BY ELLEN HARTIGAN (1861)*

Ochra Soup
[1861]

Boil a leg of veal with about four dozen ochras, an hour, then add six tomatoes, six small onions, one green pepper, a bunch of thyme and parsley, and let it boil till dinner-time. Season it with salt and red pepper to your taste, and, if agreeable, add a piece of salt pork which has been previously boiled. The soup should boil seven or eight hours.

When the U.S. Civil War began, the Union rushed to blockade Confederate shipping. White planters on the Sea Islands, fearing an invasion by the US naval forces, abandoned their plantations and fled to the mainland. When Union forces arrived on the Sea Islands in 1861, they found the Gullah people eager for their freedom, and eager as well to defend it. Many Gullahs served with distinction in the Union Army's First South Carolina Volunteers. The Sea Islands were the first place in the South where slaves were freed. The Gullah people retained many of their African foods, having brought recipes and even seeds with them. Gullah rice dishes called "red rice" and "okra soup" are similar to West African "jollof rice" and "okra soup". Jollof rice is a style of cooking brought by the Wolof people of West Africa.

10 year old Jimmie Been shucking oysters in Bluffton, South Carolina.

Oysters

WHAT TO EAT, AND HOW TO COOK IT: CONTAINING OVER ONE THOUSAND RECEIPTS BY PIERRE BLOT (1863)

Oysters.

Take one hundred and fifty oysters, put them into a saucepan, and add salt to your taste, set it on hot coals, and allow the oysters to simmer till they are heated all through, but not to boil; then take out the oysters and put them into a stone jar, leaving the liquor in the saucepan; add to it a pint of clear strong vinegar, a large teaspoonful of blades of mace, three dozen whole cloves, and three dozen whole pepper corns. Let it come to a boil, and when the oysters are quite cold in the jar pour the liquor upon them.

Oysters have long been an epicurean delight for residents of the New England colonies as well as the Deep South. While the north states tend to get their quality oysters from the Atlantic Coast or the Chesapeake Bay, the south has its own treasury trove of oysters too in the Apalachicola Bay. While not as well known as the Chesapeake, the Apalachicola River is a free-flowing river fed by the Flint and Chattahoochee Rivers of North Georgia. Joining at Lake Seminole on the Georgia/Florida line they were once one of the busiest commercial arteries in the ante-bellum south. The nutrient heavy silt is carried down the Apalachicola to the bay and sets up the perfect environment for the many oyster beds.

Peas Pudding

CONFEDERATE RECEIPT BOOK
BY WEST AND JOHNSTON, RICHMOND (1863)

> PEAS PUDDING.—Take about three quarters of a pint of split peas, and put them into a pint basin, tie a cloth over them (to give room to swell,) put them into *boiling water*, and let them boil two hours, then take them up, untie them, add an egg, beaten up, a little butter, with salt and pepper, then beat up, tie up again, and place them in the water to boil for about twenty minutes more, you will then have a well flavored and nice shaped pudding.

Agricultural practices on the small farm, which typically ranged in size from 120 to 160 acres, varied from purely pastoral to a combination of pastoral, crop, and garden farming. Hunting and gathering provided an important supplement to family food provisions. A farmer with 120 acres might be expected to use 100 acres for unfenced cattle and hog raising, firewood gathering, and hunting. Of the remaining twenty acres, ten to twelve would ordinarily be devoted to corn, a staple for both human beings and farm animals. An acre or less might be used variously for sweet sorghum or sugarcane, a fruit orchard, home garden and herb plot, and tobacco. Cash income, always minimal, came from the cultivation and harvest of two or three acres of cotton. Peas, specifically field peas, were planted not so much for food, but to capture nitrogen and return it into the soil as a replenishing fertilizer after the nutrient-draining cash crops such as cotton and corn had exhausted the soil.

Pepper Sauce

THE COMPLETE COOK.
SANDERSON (1864)

Pepper Sauce.

Take twenty-five peppers, without the seeds, cut them pretty fine, then take more than double the quantity of cabbage, cut like slaw, one root of horseradish grated, a handful of salt, rather more than a tablespoonful of mustard-seed, a tablespoonful of cloves, the same of allspice, ground; simmer a sufficient quantity of vinegar to cover it, and pour over it, mixing it well through.

"Americans can eat garbage, provided you sprinkle it liberally with ketchup, mustard, chili sauce, Tabasco sauce, cayenne pepper, or any other condiment which destroys the original flavor of the dish"

— Henry Miller

Pepper sauce was a foot soldier's best friend when it came to stomaching some of the tainted meat served to him during the war. Due to lack of refrigeration techniques, meat was often times slightly spoiled before it was ever served to the troops. Many the solider carried his own pepper sauce bottles with him to mask the rotten taste of rancid meat, especially during the hot and humid months of summer. While many men carried homemade versions of pepper sauce in cylindrical bottles, it was available to buy from stores as early as 1859.

Pickled Green Tomatoes

THE HOME MANUAL, OR, THE ECONOMICAL COOK AND HOUSE-BOOK
BY ELIZABETH NICHOLSON (1865)

> **To Pickle Green Tomatoes.**
>
> Slice one peck of green tomatoes, take one gallon of vinegar, six tablespoonsful of whole cloves, four of alspice, two of salt, one of mace, and one of cayenne pepper; boil the vinegar and spices together ten minutes, put in the tomatoes, and let all boil together about a quarter of an hour; when cold put them in jars.

Measurements in old recipes have often times been difficult to translate for modern audiences due to the terminology or ingredients used being antiquated or outdated. One term that most city-dwelling folks may have heard of but not be aware of what it means is "peck." This recipe calls for a peck of tomatoes and that may have some scratching their head as to exactly how many that is. A peck officially is a unit of dry volume or capacity that is equal to 8 quarts, 2 gallons or 537.6 cubic inches. Unofficially, it's a bushel or simply quite a few. The British "peck" is a slight bit more if you're reading an international recipe, so keep that in mind.

PICOLLILLY

THE HOME MANUAL, OR, THE ECONOMICAL COOK AND HOUSE-BOOK
BY ELIZABETH NICHOLSON (1865)

> **PICOLLILLY.**
>
> Take of cut cucumbers, beans and cabbage each six quarts; of cut peppers and small onions three quarts each; horseradish one quart—green them with vinegar and water, then put them in strong vinegar, seasoned with mustard, mustard-seed and ground cloves; add of celery and nasturtions each four quarts.

Picollilly or Picalilli is a type of relished that is made up of chopped pickled vegetables such as cucumbers, beans and cabbage and spices. Dependent upon the region, the recipe varies. In the mid-west, it is common for this relish dish to be made using gherkins. While in the northeast, the piccalilli gets its flavor from sweet peppers, both green and red. The north's version is similar to sweet pepper relish and is a popular toping on hamburgers. The south doesn't have a picollilly per se. Instead, it has Chow-Chow, a relish that uses green tomatoes, onions cabbage and green beans. The picallilli gets its bright yellow coloring from the mustards used to combine the pickled vegetables. The various recipes were probably derived from a British version that utilizes cauliflower and vegetable marrow.

Pigeons in Jelly

THE AMERICAN HOME COOK BOOK: WITH SEVERAL HUNDRED EXCELLENT RECIPES (1864)

Pigeons in Jelly.

Make some jelly of calf's foot, or if you have the liquor in which a knuckle of veal has been boiled, it will answer the same purpose; place in a stew-pan with a bunch of sweet herbs, a blade of mace, white pepper, slices of lean bacon, some lemon peel, and the pigeons, trussed and their necks propped up to make them appear natural, and stuffed with salt oysters. Bake them; when they are done, remove them from the liquor, but keep them covered close, that their colour may be preserved. Remove the fat, boil the whites of a couple of eggs with the jelly to clear it, and strain it; this is usually done by dipping a cloth into boiling water, and straining it through it, as it prevents anything like scum or dirt sweeping through the strainer. Put the jelly rough over and round the pigeons. Young chickens are nice if done in the same manner. This is a supper dish, as it is served cold.

This dish mentions in the recipe that it's considered a supper dish because it's served cold. In the antebellum south, there were two post-breakfast meals, dinner and supper. Long has been the argument over the difference between dinner and supper and the one agreed upon point is that dinner is normally the larger meal of the day. In households, both north and south, that had servants or slaves, three meals a day were expected to be prepared, so dinner in these households tended to be the last meal of the day. However, in working class homes where the wife did all the cooking herself, dinner was at midday (around 2:00 pm) for reasons of practicality. It was hard work to keep a stove fire going all day long and a waste of resources.

PILLAFF

THE AMERICAN HOME COOK BOOK: WITH SEVERAL HUNDRED EXCELLENT RECIPES (1864)

PILLAFF—AN ORIENTAL DISH.

Take a leg of mutton, cut off the meat into small slices, put them into a pan with a good sized lump of butter and fry them a light brown. With the remainder of the meat and bone make a rich soup, by pouring on three quarts of cold water and letting it simmer three hours, tightly covered. The meat must not be fried until the soup is nearly done. Put into the soup ten skinned, sliced tomatoes, three thinly sliced onions, fried a light brown, and a small piece of garden pepper—it is strong and requires but little—salt to the taste. About half an hour before the soup is done, add a large tea cup full of well washed rice, stirring it all constantly until cooked – then put in the slices of fried meat; let it simmer for five minutes. When properly prepared, the grains of rice are all whole but cooked. Cold roast beef is equally as good as mutton for a pillaff. Serve hot.

Some of the earliest references to pilaf or pilau rice can be found when studying the history of Alexander the Great as it was served to him upon capturing Marakanda. He and his army brought the dish back to Macedonia and it spread through out Europe. Since the 1800s, the spelling has changed to 'pilaf' but the dish is still basically the same. While most people know of rice pilaf, they may not know that a pilaf is actually considered a steamed rice dish that often has a meat, seafood or vegetable added to it in a seasoned broth. It's considered a Middle Eastern or Indian dish and the word its self comes from Turkish heritage. In the south, a New Year's Day combination of ham, rice and black-eyed peas is a popular dish that supposedly brings good luck to those who eat it on the first day of the year.

Plain Pound Cake

THE COMPLETE CONFECTIONER, PASTRY-COOK AND BAKER
ELEANOR PARKINSON (1864)

> **PLAIN POUND CAKE.**
>
> Cream a pound of fresh butter, and work into it a pound of crushed sugar, till quite smooth; beat nine eggs, the whites and yolks separately, and add them by degrees to the butter and sugar, and beat them together twenty minutes; then beat in, gradually, one pound of flour. Put it in a mould, and bake in a moderate oven one hour.
>
> Plum cake is made as the foregoing, only, after you have beaten it sufficiently, you add two pounds of raisins, stoned, and one pound of currants.

"If the people have no bread, let them eat cake."

— Marie Antoinette

As the war progressed and basic ingredients became scarce, cakes would only be baked on holidays such as Christmas. In the case of this tasty pound cake, 9 eggs would have been seen as extremely extravagant for the time. In fact, eggs were so rare in the camp life of a solider, that if they did obtain them, they were used for protein instead of something so indulgent as a cake. Eggs were begged, traded and even stolen from local farmhouses on a regular basis by soldiers of both camps. When cooking this egg-laden cake, remember that the Civil War era eggs were half the size of eggs today. So, if trying this recipe at home, be sure to use small or medium sized eggs in your recipe.

Plum Pudding

MRS. BEETON'S DICTIONARY OF EVERYDAY COOKERY
BY ISABELLA BEETON (1865)

Many wonder about this delicious culinary favorite that does not sport any plums in it's list of ingredients. The mystery goes back the 1600s when plums really meant raisins or other fruits like prunes. The terms were used interchangeably, even in the Oxford English Dictionary that stated a plum was " a dried grape or raisin as used for puddings cakes, etc." Noted as one of the finest culinary creations to come out of England, this sweet treat was actually outlawed in England for a while during the Puritan stronghold because it was so "sinfully rich." Thankfully, when the recipe came to America, it wasn't outlawed, but celebrated and even eventually renamed Christmas pudding. Tradition dictated long ago that small silver charms were to be baked in the pudding that would provide a tell-tell fortune for the year to come. A wishbone promised good luck, a silver thimble hinted at thrift and the anchor provided safe harbor. In England, these charms can still be purchased to use in your own creations.

Plum Wine

MISS LESLIE'S COMPLETE COOKERY. DIRECTIONS FOR COOKERY.
BY ELIZA LESLIE: 1858

Damson Plum Wine.

Cut the plums in half; to a gallon of the plums add one gallon of fresh water which has been rendered aromatic by cloves; this is done by putting two ounces of cloves into a bag and boiling in the water, and then removing the bag; to this proportion of water and fruit, add two pounds of brown sugar; let this ferment four or five days, then clarify with the whites of eggs or isinglass, then bottle up; in two weeks it is fit for use, and if rightly prepared is very palatable.

Because plum wine is historically an Irish favorite, it's no wonder the fruit wine took hold in America during the 1800s when the wave of Irish immigrants coming across the big pond was at its peak. In Ireland, it's almost a national pastime, the making of plum wine. As easy as it is to turn fruits into pies, so it is to turn fruits into wines with the quick, simple and enjoyable hobby of wine making. Land was plentiful in the 1800s and many residents enjoyed orchards or even just a plum tree or two, to kick start their winemaking hobbies. The timetable on a batch of wine would run about four months allowing for a good bottle to be enjoyed over the holidays.

Popovers

TIT-BITS OR HOW TO PREPARE A DISH AT A MODERATE EXPENSE
BY MRS. HOOPER, 1864

> One quart of milk, four eggs, one large spoonful of melted butter, a little salt, and flour enough to make a pretty thick batter. Heat your pop-over pans, which come on purpose, butter them well, and pour in the batter.

Popovers are an egg-based, hollow roll that is shaped like a muffin. Due to its hollow nature, it is perfect for filling with butter, cheese or meat. It is an especially easy way to fix breakfast or to send the men off to battle with a snack. Popovers have the added benefit bread-like but not requiring any leavening agent other than the egg. By the 1870s, Popovers were popular enough to have been included in Annie Frost's "The Godey's Lady's Book Receipts and Household Hints," as well as many other publications. For those of you who know what Yorkshire Pudding is, these are like individual Yorkshire Puddings.

Above is Mrs. Hooper's Popover recipe from "Tit-Bits or How to Prepare a Dish at a Moderate Expense," a publication printed in 1864 in both Boston and New York. Other, similar recipes were printed from 1859.

Porter Beer

THE BREWER: A FAMILIAR TREATISE ON THE ART OF BREWING
WILLIAM LOFTUS (1863)

> From this candid and open statement of the articles used in Porter, every person may adopt the plan proposed by this Treatise of brewing for himself. It will naturally happen, that those who are unacquainted with the mysteries of Porter brewing will be surprised at some of the articles, but for their information I will follow the receipts with a particular description of each article, that every person may chuse his own ingredients, and increase or decrease their proportions, as may best suit his taste, opinion or convenience.——
>
> For the benefit of those who live in lodgings, I shall add a calculation for 1 peck of Malt.——
>
> **Porter Receipt**
>
> | | Dol. Cts. |
> |---|---|
> | 1 Peck of Malt | 25 |
> | 1 lb. of Liquorice Root | 33 |
> | ⅛ oz. of Spanish Liquorice | 1 |
> | ¼ lb. of Essentia | 4 |
> | ¼ lb. of Colour | 4 |
> | ¼ lb. of Treacle | 4 |
> | ¼ lb. of Hops | 4 |
> | Capsicum, Heading, Ginger, Linseed &c. &c. | 5 |
> | Water for 6 Gallons Porter. | |
> | D. | 80 |

When the U.S. Civil War began, the Union rushed to blockade Confederate shipping. White planters on the Sea Islands, fearing an invasion by the US naval forces, abandoned their plantations and fled to the mainland. When Union forces arrived on the Sea Islands in 1861, they found the Gullah people eager for their freedom, and eager as well to defend it. Many Gullahs served with distinction in the Union Army's First South Carolina Volunteers. The Sea Islands were the first place in the South where slaves were freed. The Gullah people retained many of their African foods, having brought recipes and even seeds with them. Gullah rice dishes called "red rice" and "okra soup" are similar to West African "jollof rice" and "okra soup". Jollof rice is a style of cooking brought by the Wolof people of West Africa.

Potato Pudding

*HANDWRITTEN FAMILY RECIPE
CIVIL WAR ERA*

Joshua Leffingwell was an architect and builder in Hartford, Connecticut. Leffingwell kept a journal not just as a diary, but of helpful tidbits of information. It's seems that he also enjoyed wintering in a warmer climate. According to the Leffingwell record, Joshua and his brother, John, built a number of buildings, including the Hartford Bank, Center Church, and the Old State House. When not involved in the large projects, Joshua Leffingwell constructed houses, disassembled them, and shipped them to Trinidad. He then spent the winter reassembling them on that sunny, warm, Caribbean island. In addition, numerous recipes and household remedies have been entered in the volume. Some are directly written in, others are sewn or pinned in. Most are handwritten, though others are from newspapers. Among the various entries are a "receipt to make a beautiful and lasting whitewash," a remedy for curing an inflamed cow, recipes for seasoning sausages, Washington Cake, and keeping meat in warm weather. The above recipe is his for Potato pudding.

145

Pumpkin Pie

HANDWRITTEN FAMILY RECIPE
CIVIL WAR ERA

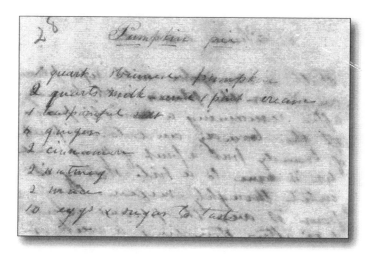

For many people, preparing for Thanksgiving and the upcoming holiday season meant many hours in the kitchen cooking. Courtesy of Texan Anna Gibbs McKinney, this is her recipe for Pumpkin Pie, from her cookbook of 1843. Anna's cookbook contains approximately seventy-five recipes that, according to the published edition of the book, she collected "from friends, relatives and newspapers and laboriously hand-copied" in ink. In addition to containing directions for cakes and other desserts, the cookbook also includes recipes for breads and biscuits, directions for making condiments and preserves, and a "recipe for curing meat by a New Orleans pork packer." Mrs. McKinney also gathered other homemaking information in her book, specifically instructions for making soap and candles as well as remedies for conditions such as smallpox, mites and vermin, cancer, sore legs, bites from poisonous insects, and "nails in the foot of man or horse."

Rabbit and Oyster Fricasee

THE GOURMET'S GUIDE TO RABBIT COOKING
GEORGIANA HILL (1859)

Chesapeake [...] more. The oyster Bay's bounty of [...] beds nearby, and fish and shellfish [...] the city's growing amazed and delighted early [...] population of workers and rail travelers. Oysters [...] connections, made were first among the bay's wonders, described as "very large and delicate in taste" and thriving in "whole banks and beds." Until the 1800s, most Chesapeake oysters were harvested for local consumption. By the mid-1800s, shucked oysters could be packed in ice or canned for shipment to distant markets. As American cities grew, demand for oysters surged, and Chesapeake oysters found ready markets in Pittsburgh, Detroit, Minneapolis, and points west. By the 1840s, oyster canning was an established industry in Baltimore the center of canning in the country. Thomas Kensett, an Englishman, began canning food in New York in the 1810s. His son and namesake was one of the first to process oysters in Baltimore, beginning in 1849. For generations, watermen and their families made a living from the local waters. No church supper, community festival, or Thanksgiving feast was complete without oysters stewed, fried, steamed, raw, or baked into a pie.

Republican Fruit Cake

One pound butter, 1 pound flour or more if needed, 1 pound sugar 1 pint molasses 1 pint sour cream 1 glass wine 1 glass brandy 10 eggs 1 tablespoon soda 2 tablespoon cinnamon, 1 tablespoon cloves 1 tablespoon mace, 1 nutmeg 3 pounds English currants ¼ pound citron 1 pound raisins roll the raisins in flour they will keep for a year. Bake one hour This will make three good loaves and I do not think you will be ashamed to place it before the Editor

Delicate Cake

Three and a half cups of sweet flour, two of sugar half cup of sweet milk, white of six eggs beaten to a froth one teaspoon cream tartar one tablespoon

Republican Fruit Cake

HANDWRITTEN FAMILY RECIPE
CIVIL WAR ERA

The ancient Romans made a mishmash of barley, pomegranate seeds, nuts and raisins as a sort of energy bar; however the modern fruitcake can be traced back to the Middle Ages as dried fruits became more widely available and fruited breads entered Western European cuisine. But variations on the fruitcake started springing up: Italy's dense, sweet-and-spicy panforte (literally, "strong bread") dates back to 13th century Sienna; Germany's stollen, a tapered loaf coated with melted butter and powdered sugar that's more bread-like in consistency, has been a Dresden delicacy since the 1400s and has its own annual festival; and then there's black cake in the Caribbean Islands, a boozy descendant of Britain's plum pudding where the fruit is soaked in rum for months, or even as long as a year. The tradition of making fruitcakes for special occasions such as weddings and holidays gained in popularity in the 18th and 19th centuries and due to the cost of the materials, it was a grand indulgence. But, as with many traditions, how this confection came to be exclusively associated with Christmas season is a mystery.

BILL OF FARE
OF THE
Presidential Inauguration Ball
IN THE
CITY OF WASHINGTON, D. C.,
On the 6th of March 1865.

Oyster Stews ....
Terrapin " ....
Oysters, pickled ....

BEEF.
Roast Beef ....
Filet de Beef ....
Beef à-la-mode ....
Beef à l'anglais ....

VEAL.
Leg of Veal ....
Fricandeau ....
Veal Malakoff ....

POULTRY.
Roast Turkey ....
Boned   " ....
Roast Chicken ....
Grouse, boned and roast ......

GAME.
Pheasant ....
Quail ....
Venison ....

PATETES.
Patète of Duck en gelée ......
Patète de fois gras ....

SMOKED.
Ham ....
Tongue en gelée ....
  do   plain ....

SALADES.
Chicken ....
Lobster ....

Ornamental Pyramides.
Nougate ....
Orange ....
Caramel with Fancy Cream Candy
Cocoanut ....
Macaroon ....

Croquant ....
Chocolate ....
Tree Cakes ....

CAKES AND TARTS.
Almond Sponge ....
Belle Alliance ....
Dame Blanche ....
Macaroon Tart ....
Tart à la Nelson ....
Tarte à l'Orleans ....
  do à la Portugaise ....
  do à la Vienne ....
Pound Cake ....
Sponge Cake ....
Lady Cake ....
Fancy small Cakes ....

JELLIES AND CREAMS.
Calfsfoot and Wine Jelly .....
Charlotte à la Russe ....
  do   do   Vanilla ....
Blanc Mangue ....
Crême Neapolitane ....
  do à la Nelson ....
  do Chateaubriand ....
  do à la Smyrna ....
  do do Nesselrode ....
Bombe à la Vanilla ....

ICE CREAM.
Vanilla ....
Lemon ....
White Coffee ....
Chocolate ....
Burnt Almonds ....
Maraschino ....

FRUIT ICES.
Strawberry ....
Orange ....
Lemon ....

DESSERT.
Grapes, Almonds, Raisins, &c.

Coffee and Chocolate.

Furnished by **G. A. BALZER**, Confectioner,
Cor. 9th & D Sts., Washington, D. C.

Republican Inaugural Ball

SMITHSONIAN MAGAZINE
BY MEGAN GAMBINO (1/15/2013)

President Abraham Lincoln's second inaugural ball was a fête to behold. On the evening of March 6, 1865 (two days after the inauguration), men escorted their ladies, one on each arm—the $10 ticket admitted three—up a grand staircase. They ascended to the top-floor hall of the Patent Office Building in Washington, D.C., now the site of the Smithsonian American Art Museum and National Portrait Gallery.

There, according to estimates, some 4,000 revelers danced quadrilles, waltzes and Virginia reels. Surely, the energy in the room spiked when the president arrived with his wife, Mary Todd Lincoln, at 10:30 p.m. The president was dressed in a dapper black suit and white gloves. Mrs. Lincoln, with jasmine and violets woven in her hair, wore a white satin off-the-shoulder gown. But, the party reached a fever pitch at the stroke of midnight, when an elaborate buffet was served. Oysters, roast beef, veal, turkey, venison, smoked ham, lobster salad and a seemingly endless display of cakes and tarts spread across a table 250 feet long. The hungry crowd charged the food, and the lavish event devolved into somewhat of a mess. "In less than an hour the table was a wreck…positively frightful to behold," wrote the New York Times. Men hoisted full trays above the masses and took them back to their friends, slopping stews and jellies along the way. "The floor of the supper room was soon sticky, pasty and oily with wasted confections, mashed cake, and debris of fowl and meat," reported the Washington Evening Star.

Soldiers at Fort Granger enjoying breakfast.

Rhubarb Jam

GODEY'S LADY'S BOOK
BY LOUIS A. GODEY (1860)

> RHUBARB JAM.—To seven pounds of rhubarb add four sweet oranges and five pounds of sugar. Peel and cut up the rhubarb. Put in the thin peel of the oranges and the pulp, after taking out the seeds and all the whites. Boil all together for one hour and a half.
>
> Godey's Lady's Book 1861, Pg. 555

The rhubarb is a very old plant that has a history of both medicinal and edible exploits. Marco Polo reports about this plant at length in his recollections of traveling through the country of China. It was reported as having been planted in Italy around 1608 and came to England in the late 1700s. America got her chance to try the Rhubarb when a Maine gardener obtained either seed or root stock from Europe around 1800 and by 1822, it was being sold in produce markets around New England. Rhubarb is a tart, red vegetable that is eaten like a fruit although it is rare that it's ever eaten raw, like an apple. When sugar is added to mixture, the refreshing result makes wonderful jams and pies.

A slave threshing rice in a sweetgrass basket in South Carolina.

Rice Cake

TIT-BITS: OR, HOW TO PREPARE A NICE DISH AT A MODERATE EXPENSE
SG KNIGHT:(1864)

RICE CAKE.

Beat the yolks of fifteen eggs, for twenty minutes; put in ten ounces of crushed sugar, half a pound of ground rice, a little brandy, two lemon-peels, grated, the whites of seven eggs, beaten to a stiff froth, and stir the whole together for a quarter of an hour. Put it in a mould, and bake it in a quick oven half an hour.

Rice was a staple food in the south prior to the War, with Georgia and the Carolinas producing the majority of the rice in the country. This rice production hit a major halt during the war and when the smoke cleared, the production of rice in America had been taken over by Louisiana where the successful use of improved machinery made the state the King of Rice in America. Carolina planters even knew which African ethnic groups were expert in rice growing and explicitly favored them in their purchases of new slaves. A newspaper in Charleston, for example, advertised the sale of 250 slaves "from the Windward and Rice Coast, valued for their knowledge of rice culture."

The knowledge system Carney describes called for different roles and distinctive kinds of expertise for men and women, and these aspects of rice culture were also transported to the New World. The importance of these skills enabled slave traders to command higher prices for women in Carolina rice-growing areas than in other American slave markets.

Five generations of slaves in Beaufort, South Carolina.

Sally Lunn

*MONDAY MORNING, HOW TO GET THROUGH IT
BARBARA HUTTON (1863)*

> **SALLY LUNN.**
>
> Cut into warmed milk a large spoonful of good butter, when quite cool add one quart of sifted flour, three eggs well beaten, one teaspoonful of soda dissolved in a little milk; beat this all together well, and add a little salt; when quite light pour into pans and bake in a quick oven.

Often confused with the Bath Bun, a Sally Lunn is a yeast bread that does indeed originate from Bath, England. For as many people that eat them, there are recipes for this delicious light bread. It is often lemon scented and is traditionally sliced horizontally and then spread with butter and put back together. There are several stories surrounding how the name of the bread came to be including the story that a Sally Lunn arrived in 1680 Bath and worked in a bakery, selling her original buns for take out or dine in. Still others believe that the name is actually French and comes from "soleil lune" or sun and moon because of the shape and look of the roll.

Soldier with a meat saw and family in the camp.

Salt Pork

*DIRECTIONS FOR COOKING BY THE TROOPS
BY FLORENCE NIGHTINGALE (1861)*

TO COOK SALT BEEF OR PORK.

Put the meat, cut in pieces of from 3 to 4 lbs., to soak the night before: in the morning wash in fresh water, and squeeze well with the hands to extract the salt; after which, put in your kettle with a pint of water to each pound, and boil from 2 to 3 hours.

Today's solider is used to standing in a mess line for his breakfast, lunch or dinner, but during the 1860s when Civil War soldiers, both northern and southern, took time to eat, it was with uncooked rations that were handed out by the Commissary departments. While some officers and Generals had the luxury of a cook to prepare their meals, it fell upon the common solider to fix his own. Because the foods had to travel well over long distances, the foods had to be easily preserved. That's why salted meat, especially pork, as unsavory as it was then- with its hair, skin and dirt left attached, was the main source of protein for most soldiers. While many soldiers referenced eating bacon in letters home, historians today believe they were referring to salted and smoked pork instead. Smoked beef was eaten only when absolutely necessary.

**Jones Dairy Farm Sausage Co.
was founded using a pre-Civil War recipe.**

THE WISCONSIN STATE JOURNAL
Sunday, July 18, 1926

Aunt Sally Crane's Recipe The Foundation for Jones "Little Pig Sausage" Industry

By CATHERINE COLBURN

AWAY back in 1836, Milo Jones the First left his Vermont home and entered the Northwest Territory as a government surveyor. His work took him into the wilds of Wisconsin, Michigan and Iowa. Of all this territory, no spot seemed so fair to him as the beautiful Rock River valley. So attractive did this region appear, and so full of promise, that a year or two later he took out a government claim, sent east for his wife and children to join him, and where the city of Fort Atkinson now stands, he laid the foundation for his future home.

He laid the foundation also for the future Jones Dairy Farm and its famous "Little Pig Sausage", the production of which has been the family pride for four generations and which now enjoy nation wide distribution and popularity. This is the story of how the tradition established by Aunt Sally Crane, Milo Jones' pioneer wife, in the savory sausages which she made and served to family friends, and wayfarers in those sturdy pioneer days, has been upheld through the years. The making of sausages of unusual quality became the family occupation as well as its pride. Today, they are produced in a large modern plant situated on the Jones Dairy Farm just outside Fort Atkinson, but they are made according to the same old recipe that Aunt Sally Crane used in the days of territorial Wisconsin.

Paid in Gold

When Grandfather Jones as Milo Jones the First is called, paid for his Wisconsin farm in '36, he used gold pieces which he had brought with him from Vermont in wooden buckets with iron lids. Grandfather Jones believed that every farm should be self supporting and consequently his Wisconsin farm soon contained a brickyard, a blacksmith shop a tannery and a tavern. Small wonder then with such a settlement, and in those days of hardship and peril when every home was of necessity an open house to all travellers that Aunt Sally's home made pork sausages should become widely known and liked. Made from an old family recipe brought with her from Vermont, these sausages called for young pig pork, home ground spices, and salt in just the right proportions.

For her doughnuts, almost as much as for her sausages, Aunt Sally was particularly famed. In olden days, the pioneer women did not always use lard for all of their cooking. The story is told that the Joneses were entertaining the terri-

Sausage

WHAT TO DO WITH THE COLD MUTTON…OTHER…GENTLEMAN OF MODERATE INCOME: (1865)

Sausage Meat.

Chop four pounds of nice clean pork very finely, one pound of good veal also chopped very finely, and season this with a large spoonful of finely rubbed sage, a teaspoonful of sweet marjoram, two dozen pounded allspice, a teaspoonful of salt, half a teaspoonful of the best cayenne pepper; mix these well together, put it in a tightly covered jar, and set it in a cool place; it is better if standing a few days. Fry it in balls a nice brown. Serve hot and free from fat.

When young men and boys joined up with the ranks of their choice, they found themselves suddenly thrust into the role of cook within their camps. No longer did they have Mamma or Sis to do the cooking for them. One of the first foods of choice was a chicken and then, a close second was a pig. While they may not know the finer arts of a stove or baking, when it comes to a dead pig, they instinctively know what to do. As the food became harder to come by, soldiers from both sides took to scavenging for food, hunting wild pigs and stealing from any neighboring farm they came across. So severe was the wipeout of pigs in this nation, five years after the war ended, the number of pigs in America was still half the number of pigs there were in the 1860 census.

GRAND REAPING.
SOUTHERN WOMEN FEELING THE EFFECTS OF REBELLION, AND CREATING BREAD RIOTS.

Southern Rolls

THE COMPLETE CONFECTIONER, PASTRY-COOK AND BAKER
ELEANOR PARKINSON (1864)

> *Or* :—To 2 lbs. of flour well dried, and 1 pint of water milk-warm, put 3 spoonsful of yeast: then knead in 2 ozs. of fresh butter and a little salt, and work all well together. The oven must be very quick, and quarter of an hour will bake them; the dough should make 12 rolls.

The Southern Bread Riots were events of civil unrest in the Confederacy on April 2, 1863. The riots were triggered mainly by foraging armies, both Union and Confederate, who ravaged crops and devoured draft animals. It was far more profitable for plantation owners to grow cotton and tobacco instead of food. The taxes on clerks, apothecaries and teachers were a mere 2% while taxes on agricultural produce were 10%. This created obvious tensions between differing classes and robbed the farmer of his income and means of providing for his family. Because of this, food crops suffered tremendously through supply and demand. The staggering inflation created by the Confederate government was also a primary cause. The drought of 1862 created a poor harvest that did not yield enough in a time when food was already scarce. From 1861 to 1863, the price of wheat tripled and butter and milk prices quadrupled. Salt, which at the time was the only practical meat preservative, was very expensive (if available at all) as a result of the Union blockade and the capture of Avery Island by the Union, which was the Confederate's largest supply of salt.

Split Pea Soup

THE ART AND MYSTERY OF CURING, PRESERVING, AND POTTING ALL KINDS OF MEATS (1864)

Split Pea Soup.

Take beef bones, or any cold meats, and two pounds of corned pork; pour on them a gallon of hot water, and let them simmer three hours, removing all the scum. Boil one quart of split pease two hours, having been previously soaked, as they require much cooking; strain off the meat and mash the pease into the soup; season with black pepper, and let it simmer one hour; fry two or three slices of bread a nice brown, cut into slices and put into the bottom of the tureen, and on them pour the soup.

It seems split pea soup is another addition to our now classic staples from our European immigrants, this time from Germany. Although pea soups have been made since the days of the Greeks and the Romans, it's a very common dish in Germany with the addition of bacon, sausage or ham. One of the very first instant food products was a pea soup that consisted of pea meal and beef fat, sold in 1867. When the Franco-Prussian war erupted, it was even trailed as the sole food fed to the soldiers along with dark bread. The pea soups never became quite as popular in America as Germany, but it is a much bigger hit in the Northeast and New England areas due to the influence of the French-Canadians who worked in the mills in the 1800s.

A Confederate letter home, describing camp rations and cooking

given Longstreet a severe punishing. Well I had to stop & eat my Supper. I tell you we had a tiptop one, it consisted of a Johnny Cake baked in an old fashioned Bake Kettle, Coffee & Bacon. It was a Supper good enough for a King. I am becoming quite an expert in the Science of Cooking, especially of the kinds of Grub furnished a Soldier. You ask what are the prospects of getting a furlough. I think they are poor. There are so many of the old regiments reenlisting in the Veteran Service & are all having furloughs allowed them, that I hardly think we will get any this winter. Well when I get to go home I want to

Sweet Journey Cake

THE NATIONAL COOK BOOK
HANNAH PETERSON (1856)

> **Sweet Journey Cake.**
>
> Stir together two large spoonsful of brown sugar, and two large spoonsful of good butter, beat the yolks of three eggs, and add it to the sugar and butter, then grate half a nutmeg, add an equal proportion of corn meal and flour to knead it, then spread it on a board, and glaze it with the white of an egg. Bake before the fire as other journey cake.

As it is today with corn bread, there are sweet and plain varieties to choose from. So was the case with the Journey cake or Johnny Cakes of the Civil War era. The sweet version was primarily used as a dessert versus the un-sweet version that was used along side a meal. While it's thought that the original Johnny cake got it's start in the Northeast/New England sector, the name Journey cake seems to have been derived from the Indian word "jonakin" or "jonikin". It is also simply possible that that name stuck because it was an easy item to cook when traveling on a long journey. Soldiers on both sides of the Civil War cooked these easy treats whenever possible according to written accounts of common menu items.

WOMEN WORKERS

Sweet Potato Pone

CONFEDERATE RECEIPT BOOK
BY WEST AND JOHNSTON, RICHMOND (1863)

Sweet Potatoe Pone.

One and three-fourths of a pound sweet potatoes boiled and mashed, stir in while warm two table-spoonsful of butter, beat these well, add a little salt, three table-spoonsful of good brown sugar, then one table-spoonful of ground ginger, and beat three gills of milk, when quite light from beating pour into a buttered pan, and bake three-fourths of an hour; serve hot.

One clear indicator of a family's economic status was the maintenance of a "tater" patch. Sweet potatoes could be used to feed both animals and humans, and not having one meant dire straits. Of the many things we Americans like to credit Christopher Columbus with, one of the tastiest would have to be the introduction of the sweet potato to the North America from the island of St Thomas. The sweet potatoes were cultivated around the 1640s in Virginia although it grows much better in the warmer more tropical states. Additionally, Indians from the southern US grew sweet potatoes in the 18th century although they may have grown it earlier than that too. The taste of the sweet potato is generally preferred over Irish potatoes in the south with the reverse being the case up north.

Syllabub

AMERICAN COOKERY
AMELIA SIMMONS 1796

> To make a fine Syllabub from the Cow.
> Sweeten a quart of cyder with double refined sugar, grate nutmeg into it, then milk your cow into your liquor, when you have thus added what quantity of milk you think proper, pour half a pint or more, in proportion to the quantity of syllabub you make, of the sweetest cream you can get all over it.

Syllabub was a popular holiday drink in the United States prior to the war. Derived from the ever popular English cookbooks of the time, original recipes called for milking cream directly into a cup of cider or wine. Reportedly this action produced a foamy drink that was quite popular, in that it allowed delicate serving glasses in many china collections to be used to showcase the drink.

Of course, American inventiveness would come into play with the introduction of churns that could reproduce the delightful whipped topping the drink was known for. One of the earliest types of churns were syllabub churns used for making a dessert made from a mixture of milk or cream, wine or cider, sugar, eggs, nutmeg and cinnamon. These churns were generally designed as a tin cylinder-shaped container with a plunger style dasher having a perforated disk of some sort at the end of the handle. This was to become the precursor to our modern whipped cream.

Tomato Ketchup

*DIRECTIONS FOR COOKING BY THE TROOPS
BY FLORENCE NIGHTINGALE (1861)*

> **Tomato Ketchup.**
>
> To a half bushel of tomatoes, after they are strained through a sieve, add a quarter of an ounce of ground cloves, a quarter of an ounce of ground mace, the same of ground ginger, half the quantity of cayenne pepper, and a small tea-cup of salt; the juice must boil two-thirds away, and then the above ingredients added, after which it must boil half an hour.

While it may sound kind of obvious to readers today that your ketchup would have tomatoes in it, that hasn't always been the case. The recipe for ketchup has changed a great deal over time and it wasn't until around the 1800s that tomatoes were even added to the list of ingredients. Then, sugar wasn't added to make it a sweet chutney until well after the Civil War ended. The term ketchup actually means the extraction of one single product with spices added. The ketchup of the mid 1800s was more of a thin runny dark hued sauce that was likely to have walnuts or fermented mushrooms as an ingredient. After the Civil War, the production of commercial versions of ketchup, most notably the German producer Heinz, sky-rocketed making it a best selling item as early as the 1884.

55th New York Volunteer Infantry at Fort Gaines (1862)

Turtle

THE FRUGAL HOUSEWIFE
LYDIA MARIA FRANCIS CHILD (1830)

> *To Drefs a Turtle.*
> Fill a boiler or kettle, with a quantity of water sufficient to fcald the callapach and Callapee, the fins, &c. and about 9 o'clock hang up your Turtle by the hind fins, cut off the head and fave the blood, take a fharp pointed knife and feparate the callapach from the callapee, or the back from the belly part, down to the fhoulders, fo as to come at the entrails which take out, and clean them, as you would thofe of any other animal, and throw them into a tub of clean water, taking great care not to break the gall, but to cut it off from the liver and throw it away, then feperate each diftinctly and put the guts into another veffel, open them with a fmall pen-knife end to end,

On January 8, 1862, President and Mrs. Lincoln visited the 55th New York Volunteer Infantry at Fort Gaines, situated on a hill in farmland five miles northwest of the White House.2 For this occasion, the enlisted French chefs prepared a light afternoon meal called a "collation" which the president clearly enjoyed, saying that he had not dined so well since coming to Washington. Not surprisingly, the reputation of the regiment's cuisine quickly spread, causing many of its culinary artists to be carried off by Union Generals. The commander of the 55th later recalled, "…the fires of the kitchen saved them from the fire of the enemy," which was true, for this regiment was devastated during the large-scale offensive launched in southeastern Virginia in March of that year. Called the Gardes Lafayette, this predominantly French-immigrant regiment was known for its French Algerian-style Zouave uniforms.1 Since many of the men in this unit previously worked in the kitchens of the city's hotels and restaurants, it is not surprising that this unit became well-known for its good food.

Vegetable Soup

COOKERY FOR ENGLISH HOUSEHOLDS
MACMILLAN AND CO. LONDON AND CAMBRIDGE (1864)

> 14. *Julienne* (*Vegetable Soup*).
>
> Cut into small dice or fillets all sorts of vegetables (fresh), carrots, turnips, lettuces, cabbages, French beans, potatoes, peas, cauliflowers, onions, &c. and a little chervil. Put a quarter of a pound of fresh butter into a pan; let it melt without browning; add your vegetables, and stir them with a wooden spoon for five minutes. Be careful not to let them take colour. Fill your pan with boiling water; salt and pepper. Cover your pan with the lid, and let the soup boil until the vegetables are perfectly tender; then put two spoonfuls of rice into the soup. Mix two yolks of eggs with a small quantity of milk; pass through a silk sieve; add to your eggs three spoonfuls of thick cream, and beat it well together. Take your soup off the fire and wait till it ceases boiling; then stirring it with one hand, pour slowly into it your *liaison* of eggs and cream, and serve immediately.
>
> This soup is delicious if carefully prepared; the more variety there is in the vegetables the better it is. An intelligent cook will soon remark that vegetables with a strong taste, such as cabbages, turnips, and onions, should be used in a less proportion than potatoes or green peas.

The connection between England and the United States was quite strong at the time of the war, especially in the Southern states. English manufacturing and households highly prized the cotton and rice that formed the agricultural backbone of the Southern economy. It was hoped by the Confederacy that England would enter the war on the Southern side to protect this flow of commerce.

At the beginning of the war, Secretary of State William Seward declared the Southern ports "blockaded" as opposed to "closed", a legal technicality that allowed for interational blockade runners, most of whom were British. These profiteers supplied a range of goods from foods, weapons and even books that were no longer available from Northern sources. In fact, many of the ships used by both sides during the course of the war were built in English shipyards, along with an assortment of weapons and even uniforms.

Washington Breakfast Cake

THE IMPROVED HOUSEWIFE
A. L. WEBSTER (1847) 9TH REV

Washington Breakfast Cake.

Cut up in warm milk one spoonful of good butter; when cool, stir in one pound and one-fourth of sifted flour, two eggs well beaten, a little salt, and a large spoonful of good yeast. Mix these well together; put it into buttered tins to rise; when risen, bake three fourths of an hour.

Baked goods from home were always a welcome gift for soldiers, especially confections, as sugar was scarce for most soldiers. What our ancestors called a breakfast cake, we know today as a coffee cake. It's not a recipe that was one day invented, but developed over time into the breakfast or dessert dish that generations have enjoyed for years. Much like the plum cake that doesn't have plums, the coffee cake or breakfast cake doesn't contain coffee, as its name was assigned because everyone loved to eat their cakes with a cuppa joe. While this recipe is one of many, breakfast cakes come in a wide variety, containing an array of ingredients (none of which are coffee.) American versions are especially varied as they reflect a melting pot of recipes that came from many different countries that came together in early America. So, as John Heywood put it so well, *"Would ye both eat your cake and have your cake?"* It is suggested that yes, you should bake it and it enjoy it as both breakfast and dessert.

White Puddings

COOKERY FOR ENGLISH HOUSEHOLDS
MACMILLAN AND CO. LONDON AND CAMBRIDGE (1864)

White Puddings.

Procure the pig's blood, then add half a pound of half-boiled rice, set it to cool, keeping it stirred, add a little more rice boiled in milk, add it to the blood, cut up about one pound of fat pork into large dice, melt half a pound of lard and pour into the blood and rice, then add your fat, with a few bread crumbs, three shalots, a little parsley, some black pepper, cayenne pepper, and salt; mix all well together, then fill into skins as before; tie them the length you wish them, then boil them a quarter of an hour, take them out and lay them on some new clean straw until cold, then give them another boil for a few minutes, then turn them as before until wanted, put them in the oven when you require them, or fry them or broil them.

The Union Stock Yard & Transit Co., or The Yards, was the meatpacking district in Chicago for more than a century, starting in the 1860's. The district was operated by a group of railroad companies that acquired swampland and turned it to a centralized processing area. The Union Stockyards operated in the New City community area for 106 years, helping Chicago become known as "hog butcher for the world" and the center of the American meatpacking industry for decades. The stockyards became the focal point of the rise of some of the earliest international companies. These companies refined novel industrial innovations and influenced financial markets. Both the rise and fall of the district owe their fortunes to the evolution of transportation services and technology in America. The stockyards have become an integral part of the popular culture of Chicago's history. From the Civil War until the 1920s and peaking in 1924, more meat was processed in Chicago than in any other place in the world.

NUMBER

THE ATLANTIC ST[EAM]
OF THE CON[FEDERACY]

SHARES $1,000 EACH

This is to Certify, That
entitled to Three (3)
of The Atlantic Steam Packet Com[pany]
Transferable only at the Office
on surrender of this Certificate.

Witn[ess]

The Confederate Government even conducted stock issues

Sam¹. A. Nelson

TREASURER.

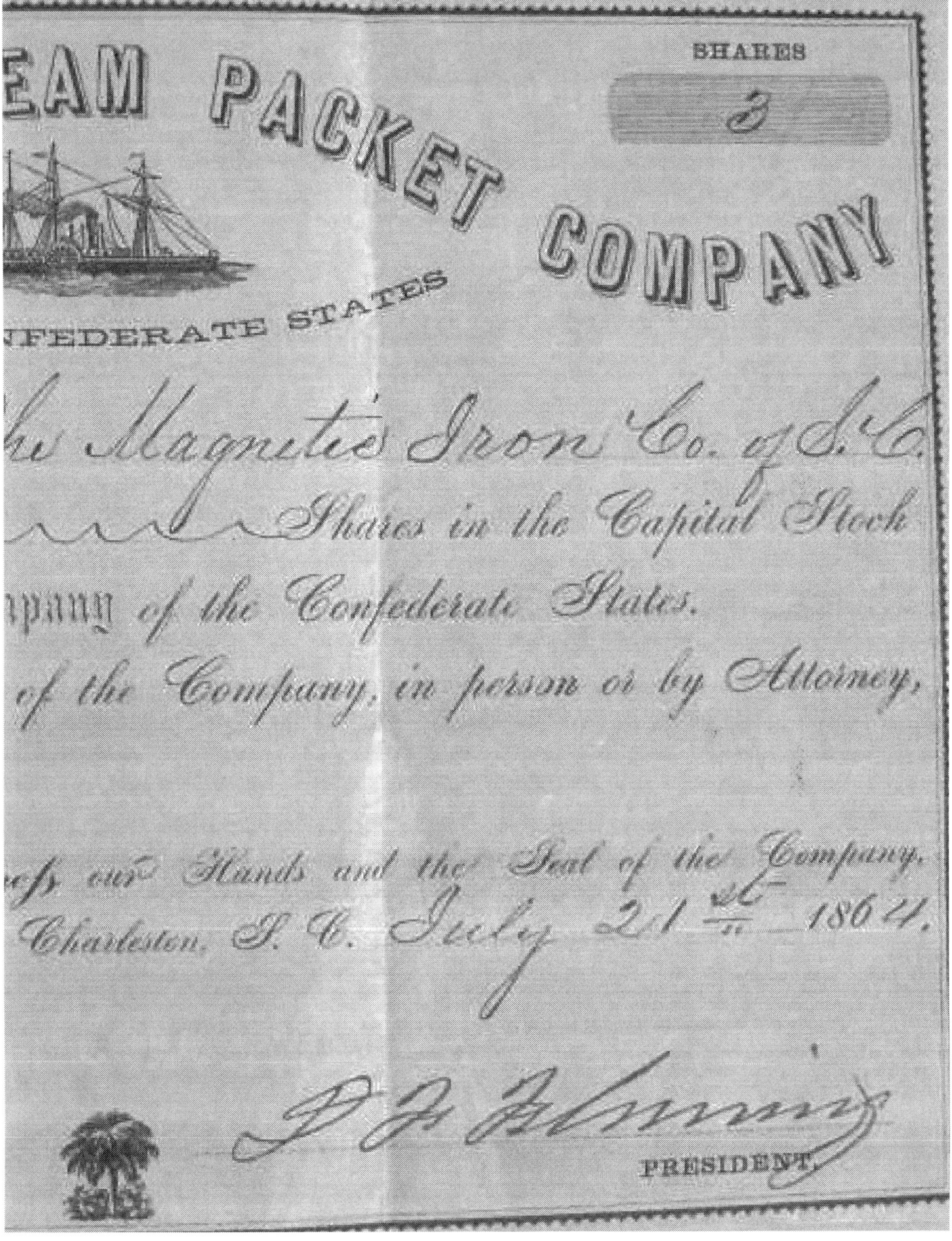

...EAM PACKET COMPANY

SHARES 3

...NFEDERATE STATES

...he Magnetic Iron Co. of S.C.

_____ Shares in the Capital Stock

...pany of the Confederate States.

...of the Company, in person or by Attorney,

...ss our Hands and the Seal of the Company,
...Charleston, S.C. July 21st 1864.

PRESIDENT

Steven W. Siler is a firefighter-cum-chef serving in Bellingham, Washington. Long marinated in the epicurean heritage of the Deep South, Steven has spent over 20 years (dear God has it been that long?!) in the much-vaulted restaurant industry from BOH to FOH to chef. In addition, he has served as an editor and contributing writer for several food publications. When not trying to shove food down his fellow firefighters' gullets, he enjoys sailing and sampling the finest of scotches and wines, and has an irrational love affair with opera. He swears one day he will relive the above picture on the Gulf Coast with a good Will.

This cookbook is the one of the first of a series of culinary celebrations from Smoke Alarm Media, based in the Pacific Northwest. Smoke Alarm Media is named for another series of unfortunate culinary accidents at an unnamed fire department, also in the Pacific Northwest. One of the founders was an active firefighter. Having been trained as a chef, he found himself in the position of cooking frequently at the fire station. Alas, his culinary skills were somewhat lacking in using the broiler and smoke would soon fill the kitchen and station. The incidents became so frequent that the 911 dispatch would call the station and ask if "Chef Smoke Alarm" would kindly refrain from cooking on his shift. Thus Smoke Alarm Media was born.

WWW.SMOKEALARMMEDIA.COM